Also by Richard Salter

Elizabeth I and her Reign

Documents and Debates
General Editor: John Wroughton M.A., F.R.Hist.S.

Peel, Gladstone and Disraeli

Richard Salter
Head of Humanities, Ladymead School, Taunton

First edition 1991

Published by
MACMILLAN EDUCATION LTD
Houndmills, Basingstoke, Hampshire RG21 2XS
and London
Companies and representatives
throughout the world

British Library Cataloguing in Publication Data
Salter, Richard
Peel, Gladstone and Disraeli – (Documents and debates).
1. Great Britain. Peel, Sir Robert, 1788–1850 2. Great Britain. Gladstone, W. E. (William Ewart) 1809–1898 3. Great Britain. Disraeli, Benjamin. Biographies
I. Title II. Series
941.081092

ISBN 0–333–48860–1

Contents

To Julie

General Editor's Preface

This book forms part of a series entitled *Documents and Debates*, which is aimed primarily at sixth formers. The earlier volumes in the series each covered approximately one century of history, using material both from original documents and from modern historians. The more recent volumes, however, are designed in response to the changing trends in history examinations at 18 plus, most of which now demand the study of documentary sources and the testing of historical skills. Each volume therefore concentrates on a particular topic within a narrow span of time. It consists of eight sections, each dealing with a major theme in depth, illustrated by extracts drawn from primary sources. The series intends partly to provide experience for those pupils who are required to answer questions on documentary material at A-level, and partly to provide pupils of all abilities with a digestible and interesting collection of source material, which will extend the normal textbook approach.

This book is designed essentially for the pupil's own personal use. The author's introduction will put the period as a whole into perspective, highlighting the central issues, main controversies, available source material and recent developments. Although it is clearly not our intention to replace the traditional textbook, each section will carry its own brief introduction, which will set the documents into context. A wide variety of source material has been used in order to give the pupils the maximum amount of experience – letters, speeches, newspapers, memoirs, diaries, official papers, Acts of Parliament, Minute Books, accounts, local documents, family papers, etc. The questions vary in difficulty, but aim throughout to compel the pupil to think in depth by the use of unfamiliar material. Historical knowledge and understanding will be tested, as well as basic comprehension. Pupils will also be encouraged by the questions to assess the reliability of evidence, to recognise bias and emotional prejudice, to reconcile conflicting accounts and to extract the essential from the irrelevant. Some questions, *marked with an asterisk*, require knowledge outside the immediate extract and are intended for further research or discussion, based on pupil's general knowledge of the period. Finally, we hope that students using this material will learn something of the nature of historical inquiry and the role of the historian.

John Wroughton

Acknowledgements

The author extends his warm thanks to Professor Norman Gash and William Maidlow for their advice, and to the staffs of Exeter University Library, Somerset Record Office, the Bodleian Library, the British Library and St Deiniol's Library, Hawarden, for their help.

The author and publishers wish to thank the following who have kindly given permission for the use of copyright material: the British Library for extracts from archive material; the John Rylands University Library of Manchester for letter from William Gladstone to William Farr, English MS 339, Farr Papers; Royal Historical Society for extracts from *Camden 3rd Series,* Vols 81, 82 and 90, 1958; Somerset County Council for extracts from archive material, Ref. DD/X/STT.

Every effort has been made to trace all the copyright holders but if any have been inadvertently overlooked the publishers will be pleased to make the necessary arrangement at the first opportunity.

Peel, Gladstone and Disraeli

John Morley, William Gladstone's supporter and biographer, remarked that only two things had ever frightened him: his first view of Dublin Castle and his first sight of the Gladstone papers. This comment reminds us not only of the shadow which Irish misery and anger cast over Victorian politics, but also of the volume of material available for the study of the period.

This mass of material is not, however, undifferentiated. In its quantity and tone it is biased towards the Liberal-Conservative 'establishment', and it is relatively difficult to balance against this the authentic voices of Irish opinion, of foreign comment and criticism or of the strivings of women and working people. In this volume I have attempted to introduce a little of this material but I am conscious of being open to the accusation of 'tokenism' – and this book is mainly a study of the main stream of politics as it was perceived at the time. Spice is added to the study by the fact that Robert Peel, Bejamin Disraeli and William Gladstone were not entirely at home in this main stream, either in respect of their origins or of their opinions.

The student must use the extracts in this book with caution for a number of reasons. First, they have been selected and edited, and this process associates them with the present author's perceptions and prejudices, as well as those of previous editors of published documents. Editing, if only for the sake of brevity, can give an important, lengthy document a tone or emphasis it does not have in its complete form, and the student is strongly advised to seek out and read documents such as Peel's Tamworth Manifesto, Disraeli's Crystal Palace speech and Gladstone's Bulgarian pamphlet in full.

The second factor is one of proximity. I have a friend still living, sound in mind, who started school before Gladstone died, and this is a reminder of the seamless continuity of history, of which the author of the last extract in the book was also aware. This renders the neat distinction between 'primary' and 'secondary' evidence invalid. The first biographies of Victorian politicians are essentially 'primary' sources, written by people who had known their subjects personally and who were variously supporters, sympathisers, enthusiasts or apologists for their subjects. But are we now so detached from the political arguments and issues of the nineteenth century that we can be sure the historians of our own day will not be tempted to take sides?

The resolution of this problem for the student is this: no document of any age is of much value in isolation; like a single flint hand-axe it is mute. Like the archaeological find it must be studied in context, and this context begins with associated contemporary documents, and widens through the subsequent decades of commentary and historical writing. When all this is weighed up the student can attempt a reconstruction of the past that is both imaginative and scholarly.

The first generation of historical writing on the Victorian age consists of the biographies to which I have already referred, such as those of Gladstone and Disraeli by Morley, Moneypenny and Buckle. To these may be added memoirs and published collections of letters and speeches. The presumption in most cases is that the work is sympathetic to the subject.

The second generation of writing, in the 1930s, contributes R.C.K. Ensor's and Sir Llewellyn Woodward's volumes of the *Oxford History of England*, which are still unsurpassed for their breadth and balance. At the same time, R.W. Seton-Watson's work on the Eastern Question and J.L. Hammond's study of Gladstone and the Irish Nation are commentaries on specific issues with wider implications, and being broadly pro-Gladstonian they provide many propositions which can be tested and challenged.

The third generation has contributed the second wave of biography, undertaken, for example, by Robert Blake, Norman Gash, Philip Magnus, John Prest and Elizabeth Longford. To these authors distance has lent a little detachment, and their sympathy for the subject cannot always be taken for granted. The same generation has contributed detailed political studies. Those of H.J. Hanham and Norman Gash have a view of a period, while others focus on one party: John Vincent, T.A. Jenkins, D.A. Hamer and D. Southgate have studied the Liberals, while Robert Blake and Paul Smith have scrutinised the Conservatives and Henry Pelling has chronicled the origins of the Labour Party. These detailed political studies have been amplified by numerous articles, and have made use, among other materials, of statistical analyses of increasing sophistication.

It would be impossible in this short book to offer comment or raise questions on the whole span of Victorian political history, let alone the wider social, economic, cultural and religious contexts. Two comments must suffice, and they are seemingly at odds. On the one hand the political agenda of, say, the 1880s seems very fresh more than a century later: Ireland, Afghanistan, South Africa, Muslim fundamentalism, Education, Local Government finance. On the other hand we must bear in mind how different are the politics of the nineteenth century from those of the twentieth, although they masquerade under many of the same names and titles. Women, and men who were not householders, were excluded from the parliamentary franchise until 1918, and in the infancy of democracy, wealth and rank were still comparatively influential. Party discipline, though developing, was much less strict than in this century. Changes in government were often brought about by 'swings' in public opinion much less marked than in this century, and to assess the significance of any election the historian must consider such factors as uncontested seats and boroughs returning two or more members. The media for public commentary and prediction have changed: for the modern opinion polls and television broadcasts substitute the pamphlet, the public meeting and the newspaper.

And so to our 'heroes', Peel, Disraeli and Gladstone. Each of them has been hailed as a great statesman by contemporary supporters and by historians, yet by comparison with some quite uncharismatic twentieth-century figures, such as Stanley Baldwin and Harold Wilson, they were not very successful. Disraeli, in particular, spent longer in opposition than any political figure of comparable stature, and none of the three ever successfully defended a majority at a general election. Yet their influence on political and social developments in and out of office, but especially during the ministries of 1841, 1868 and 1874, marks them as characters who helped to mould not just their own times but our century too.

1 Children of an Age

The three central figures in this political study share a number of points of contact to set against their divergences. Middle-class sons of an industrialist, a merchant and a literary gentleman, in an age in which the highest echelons of politics were dominated by aristocrats, they sat on the same side of the House of Commons for nine years. The arch-rivals Gladstone and Disraeli both claimed spiritual descent from George Canning. All could be (and were) accused of betrayal of party: Gladstone in the Peelite phase, Peel in both the Catholic Emancipation and the Corn Law crises, Disraeli not only in his youth but in 1867 too, when Carnarvon accused him of a political betrayal without parallel.

For each political career there is a favourable and an unfavourable interpretation between which the student must decide, given certain clues. Is Disraeli an unprincipled egoist or the visionary of Young England? A clue lies in the famous comment about the greasy pole. In a greasy pole contest one climbs to the top on the backs of, and with the consent of, the team members. Apart from his attacks on Peel, Disraeli's political activities are lacking in rancour and conspiracy.

Is Peel the betrayer of tory interests or the champion of the common people? His early career is a clue: it brought him into daily contact with the human aspects, first, of the Irish question, then of home affairs.

Gladstone's transformation from high tory to the 'People's William' also reflects a concept of duty: not in his case to a party, class or system, but to religious and personal convictions which made politics, for him, an aspect of obedience to God's will.

The student should approach the evidence for our subjects' early lives with caution. What strata of hindsight and self-justification had accumulated in the sixty years before Gladstone penned his recollections of early life? What use does the student make of the expressly self-explanatory material contained in Peel's Memoirs or Disraeli's Taunton speeches and pamphlets? How valuable is the anecdotal material in Greville's memoirs, of whom Lord John Manners remarked, 'it is like Judas Iscariot writing the lives of the Apostles'?

1 A Curious Tale

Newmarket, Sunday [3 May] 1846
[Charles] Arbuthnot told the Duke of Bedford an anecdote, which I have great difficulty in believing. It is this: that when he was at the Treasury one day [in 1812], old Sir Robert Peel called on him and said, 'I am come to you about a matter of great importance to myself, but which I think is also of importance to your Government. If you do not speedily confer high office on my son he will go over to the Whigs, and be for ever lost to the party.' He told Lord Liverpool this, who immediately made young Peel Irish Secretary. If it is true, never did any father do a greater injury to a son, for if Peel had joined a more congenial Party he might have followed the best of his political inclination, and would have escaped all the false positions in which he has been placed; instead of the insincere career that he has pursued which must have been replete with internal mortification, disgust and shame, he might have given out his real sentiments and acted upon them. He would neither have fettered nor perverted his understanding, and he would have been an abler, a better and a happier man, besides incomparably more useful to the country. As it is, his whole life has been spent in doing enormous mischief and in attempts to repair that mischief. It will be a curious biography whenever it comes to be written, but not a creditable one.

The Greville Memoirs (Charles C.F. Greville, Clerk to the Privy Council 1821–59), ed. Henry Reeve, Vol. I, 1888, p 395.

Questions

a What value can be placed on anecdotal evidence such as this? How would you set about authenticating or demolishing the main factual assertion made here?

★ *b* What factors might have discouraged Peel from joining the Whigs in 1812?

★ *c* Did this story have particular significance at the time that it was reported by Greville?

d According to Greville, what personal sacrifices and compromises had Peel made over the years?

★ *e* How balanced and fair are Greville's criticisms of Peel, as an individual contemporary? (see also Chapter 3, extract 2.)

f Is Greville's assessment of Peel's career shared by the historians you have read?

2 Pressures on Peel: the Catholic question

(a) O'Connell and County Clare

Lord Anglesey [Lord Lieutenant of Ireland] to Mr. Peel

Phoenix Park [Dublin] June 30, 1828

My dear Mr. Peel,

I have nothing particular to relate.

5 There is, in the opinion of the General Officer in command at Limerick, who has removed to Clare Castle, ample force to keep the peace and to ensure freedom of election.

I believe O'Connell and his gang are very anxious to prevent riot, if it were only with the view to show the absolute control 10 under which they have the priesthood, and by them the population. I am sorry to observe that the Bishops, many of whom are acting with much moderation, discretion and goodwill, have much less influence than I had imagined. . .

P.S. – Your letter of the 28th is this instant received.

15 Believe me, I make ample allowance for your pressure of business, and for your distress of mind at the loss of a sister. You may be quite sure that Fitzgerald will be beat. What will be said of a popular representative who, being returned for a county, does not present himself at the table of the House? I do not think O'Connell 20 is doing himself any good. I am sure he is doing the Catholic cause much injury. I fear I shall have a good deal of trouble with the Orangemen on the 12th [July].

A.

Mr. Peel to Lord Anglesey (Most Private)

25 Whitehall, July 13, 1828

[In the interval between these letters O'Connell was elected for County Clare]

My dear Lord Anglesey,

. . . A considerable difference of opinion prevails among many 30 who under ordinary circumstances would support Lord John Russell's motion [for Catholic Emancipation] as to the policy of bringing it forward at this period of the Session. Some probably think that any legislative declaration of opinion in favour of the Roman Catholics following so closely the recent events in Clare 35 would be ill-timed. I know that earnest representations have been made to Lord John against the agitation of the question at present. What effect these representations may have I know not . . . .

I apprehend it to be quite clear that Mr. O'Connell cannot possibly take his seat as a Member of Parliament. He will have no 40 opportunity of making any harangue. If he appears, the Speaker will desire him to take the oaths required by Law, and if he declines to take them will treat him as a stranger and intruder, and listen to nothing that he has to say. . . .

Memoirs of Sir Robert Peel, ed. Lord Mahon and Edward Cardwell, Part I, 1856, pp 136–7, 141–3

(b) Parental pressure

My Dear Robert,

45 Though in the Country we see through a glass darkly, I have not lately been blind to the difficulties of your unhappy situation and have found myself but ill able, with an impaired constitution, to contemplate the peculiarity of your situation without great uneasiness. In the present distracted state of Ireland with a people 50 under the dominion of the worst party feelings, generated and nursed by Governors, unfriendly to our Constitution, I fear your last concession [repeal of the Test and Corporation Acts] will only embolden resistance, and tend to widen the breach, intended by the Government to close. I trust the consciousness of your having acted 55 for the best will sustain you in every change of circumstances and enable you to cherish new friendships, without inflicting a wound on old ones. Some of your constituents may be pleased with your offer to resign your situation, as one of the representatives of the University, and boast, that the Protestant cause has sustained a 60 shock by the retirement of an able advocate. As a friend to the good old cause I trust the University will not dispense with a connexion which you have ever considered as highly honourable. I could say more but am unwilling to withdraw your attention from subjects of more importance.

65 With unabated attachment I am my Dear Robert your affectionate Father

Drayton 8 Feby. 1829 Robert Peel

British Library, Add. MS 40398, folio 204

(c) Protestant pressure

5 York Terrace, Regents Park

Feb. 7. 1829

My dear Sir,

. . . In the present state of things, it seems to me a matter of 70 duty, to declare that my political opinions are wholly unchanged. Towards my Roman Catholic fellow subjects I have ever felt and acted with kindness and goodwill: but my conviction is unalterable, that the worst consequences, civil and ecclesiastical, to England and to Ireland must arise from admitting, under any 75 modifications, the Roman Catholic body, or any part of it, to political power.

It is my sober, settled persuasion that, however it may suspend for a time, concession will remove none of the existing evils, but will greatly aggravate them all: that it may, possibly, purchase the 80 chance of a temporary calm, but with a certainty of growing and permanent troubles, involving consequences beyond human calculation or control; the melancholy commencement of which, may, not improbably, be witnessed by the present generation. . . .

40 I have the honour to be,
my dear Sir,
your obliged and faithful
humble servant.
John [Bishop of] Limerick
British Library, Add.MS. 40398, folio 190

(d) Protestants for emancipation

DECLARATION
OF THE
UNDERSIGNED PROTESTANTS
IN FAVOUR OF
A FINAL AND CONCILIATORY ADJUSTMENT OF
THE CATHOLIC QUESTION

95 We the undersigned; being personally interested in the condition, and sincerely anxious for the happiness of Ireland, feel ourselves called upon at the present juncture, to declare the conviction we entertain, that the disqualifying laws which affect his Majesty's Roman Catholic Subjects are productive of consequences prejudi-
100 cial in the highest degree to the interests of Ireland, and the Empire to which she is united. With respect to Ireland in particular, they are a primary cause of her poverty and wretchedness, and the source of those political discontents and religious animosities that distract the country, endanger the safety of its institutions, and are
105 destructive alike of social happiness and national prosperity.

We are further of opinion that unless the wisdom of the Legislature shall speedily apply a remedy to these evils, they must, in their rapid passage, assume at no distant period, such a character as must render their ultimate removal still more difficult, if not
110 impossible.

We therefore deem it of paramount importance to the welfare of the Empire at large and of Ireland especially that the whole subject should be taken into immediate consideration by Parliament, with a view to such a final and conciliatory adjustment as may be
115 conducive to the peace and strength of the United Kingdom, to the stability of our national institutions, and to the general satisfaction and concord of all classes of his Majesty's subjects.

[A long list of Irish Peers, Knights and gentlemen follows]
British Library, Add. MS 40398, folio 199

Questions

a According to Lord Anglesey, what were Daniel O'Connell's motives in wishing the County Clare election to take place peacefully?

b Explain the reference to 'trouble with the Orangemen' (extract *a*, line 22).

★ *c* With reference to extract *a*, trace the course of concessions to the Catholics in 1828 and 1829, and the positions taken by individuals in the Whig and Tory Parties.

★ *d* Did the predictions made in either extract *c* or extract *d* come true?

e What insights do these extracts provide about the conflicting pressures on Peel during the Catholic Emancipation crisis?

3 The rising hope . . .

(a) The old Gladstone remembers the young Gladstone's politics

12 July 1892

The dominant influence on my first political ideas was certainly that of Mr. Canning of whom my father, previously a supporter of the Whigs, had become a determined follower. In all matters civil and religious I was thoroughly submissive, and unquestioningly
5 believed whatever was taught me, or whatever insensibly filtered into me from my surroundings, to be right. Thus like my father I was when a boy Tory in a general way.

But this was subject in Mr. Canning and his followers to three very important heads of exception. First the subject which was by
10 far the most prominently before the public eye was that of Roman Catholic emancipation. On this I was with Canning and had no sympathy with the other party. The second concerned the beginnings of the movement towards freedom of trade, which made Mr. Huskisson (in particular) even more hateful to the Tory
15 Party than Cobden or Peel was at its completion. I remember visiting in the year 1828 a silk-manufactory at Macclesfield. The silk handkerchiefs exhibited to the visitors were then just placed in competition with French goods, subject to a protective duty of 30%. Of commercial laws I understood nothing: but the thought
20 which on the view passed distinctly through my mind was 'what wretched productions: why should the Law give factitious advantage to the sale of such commodities!' Thirdly there was the hostility of Mr. Canning to the Holy Alliance.

I was not a boy of strong political leanings. I went into the Eton
25 debating society in (I think) 1825, which was the focus of what little thought there was in the school outside our school life. but our nascent energies were repressed by a rule which the authorities had imposed and which precluded our discussing any public question which was not more than fifty years old. And I remember Dr.
30 Keate complained to me of our debating the Rohilla War of Warren Hastings because it had taken place only fifty-two years before.

But spirits keener or larger (or both) than mine were at work: and although the rule remained the great controversies of Pitt and Fox came to be debated among us (or rather some among these, for 35 I do not think we rose to the French war or the Irish union) at clandestine or irregular meetings. . . .

We were all however of a milder or sterner inclination to Toryism insofar that we rather scoffed at a somewhat heavy boy named Law, a colleger, who defended Radical principles, and who 40 was so impudent as to make the more than questionable admission that 'the Bible was a Tory book.'

I have had however an opportunity of refreshing my recollections upon the colour of my politics at this time, memory if alone being an insufficient guide. Last spring Messrs. Sotheby informed 45 me that they were commissioned to sell a mass of family papers which had belonged to Mr. W. W. Farr, a Hampshire gentleman, a contemporary and friend of mine at Eton [Gladstone requested their withdrawal from sale]. . . . They dwelt much on the proceedings of the Eton debaters, among whom he had been 50 counted: and they exhibited my opinions as Liberal I think to the full extent which Canningism allowed.

British Library, Add. MS 44790, folios 26–9, quoted in *The Prime Ministers' Papers Series: W.E. Gladstone, I. Autobiographica*, ed. John Brooke and Mary Sorensen, 1971, pp 33–4

(b) The young Gladstone speaks for himself

W. Gladstone to William Farr, Eton College, May 15th 1827

. . . To tell the truth, I do not like the present state of things. I rejoice to think that Catholic Emancipation seems now more 55 clearly in view, than it was a very short time ago: and so far, I think, we are bettered by the change. But I do not like the abuse which has been so scandalously heaped on the ex-Ministers, particularly the old Earl of Eldon. I do not like the Marchioness of Conyngham's share in the business: I do not like Canning's 60 accepting the premiership without the concession of the Catholic claims: and think it will be rather extraordinary to see His Majesty's Prime Minister, the actual head of the executive government, advocating so material a change in the formation of the constitution. That is not a situation (in my humble opinion) for an 65 emancipationist to occupy while exclusion continues. I think Lord Grey has acted, in consistency with his opinions, a very manly and honourable part; and I do not think that the Whigs can be justified in forming what so many of them have done, a thick and thin coalition with a man who differs so widely from them on reform, 70 the Corporation and Test Acts, and the line of policy which ought to be pursued towards the West Indian colonial governments by the

British. Peel has certainly acted a most manly, honourable and dignified part, and one which will raise him ever higher than he was before in the estimation of the country. . . .

75 John Rylands Library, English MS 339, quoted in *The Prime Ministers' Papers Series: W.E. Gladstone, I. Autobiographica*, op. cit., pp 189–90

Questions

a In what way does Gladstone's youthful letter reinforce or correct his later recollections?

b Comment on Gladstone's use of the terms 'Whigs', 'Tory' and 'Liberal' (extract *a*, lines 3, 7 and 50). To what extent is his use of any of these terms anachronistic?

c What evidence do these extracts provide about Gladstone's early political influences?

4 An enemy of Reform

(a) Reaction recalled

12 July 1892

This crisis [in the history of Gladstone's ideas] came with the promulgation of the plan of reform prepared by the Government of Lord Grey on March 1, 1831. My prepossessions were against Lord Grey on account of his conduct in 1827 on the Corn Bill of Mr.
5 Canning. I was charged with the Canning and Burke idea of reform. Mr. Hallam was known to be alarmed. Radicalism was delighted. Sir Walter Scott was against it: and that great magician was with me an authority in all things. Oxford was mad. I was only saved by the strong pressure of work from unchecked political
10 excitement: but this was the year of the schools [examinations], and unless for a single speech at the Union I do not think the politics even of reform were allowed dangerously to seduce my thoughts, though I remember some foolish pranks: such for example as printing at my own costs and charges some foolish anti-reform
15 placards based on the idea, then standing for gospel with anti-reformers, that simply and without qualification reform was revolution. . . .

From this epoch dates my early Toryism, and from this source it sprang. And I still go so far as to hold (but no farther) that, by
20 reason of the extraordinary peculiarities of the old system, and the then unknown nature of the region in which we were about to travel, the opposition to the first Reform Bill was less unreasonable than the opposition in subsequent years to subsequent measures, when the success of the first great experiment had been established.
25 Behold me then in a new position. On the one hand bound down

to ten or twelve hours a day of academic work – more often I think twelve then ten – on the other hand inwardly possessed with a persuasion that the Reform Bill was to be the ruin of the country.

Where lay the root of this folly? It lay here. Early education, civil or religious, had never taught me, and Oxford had rather tended to hide from me, the great fact that liberty is a great and precious gift of God, and that human excellence cannot grow up in a nation without it.

British Library, Add. MS 44790, folios 31–5, quoted in *The Prime Ministers' Papers Series: W.E. Gladstone, I. Autobiographica*, op. cit., pp 36–7

(b) Reaction expressed

People of England!

Your Parliament is dissolved for having voted on Tuesday night that the Papists of Ireland should not be permitted to return a larger proportion of Members to Parliament, than that which was solemnly established at the Union between the two countries. We add no comment: nor is any needed. Do not for a moment believe it to be an act of your beloved King.

You are called on to exercise your suffrages in favour of men who wish to establish a NEW CONSTITUTION.

Before you vote, ask yourselves the following questions, and let no man DIVERT YOUR ATTENTION FROM THEM.

1. What has *South America* gained by new constitutions? Confusion.
2. What has *France* gained by a new constitution? Disorganisation.
3. What has *Belgium* gained by a new constitution? Starvation.
4. What is 'Old England' to gain by a new constitution? and
5. What am *I* to gain by a new constitution?

Answer these for yourselves: vote for men who are solemnly pledged

1. To redress every grievance.
2. To remove every blemish.
3. TO RESIST REVOLUTION TO THE DEATH.

And may God send a happy issue!

Briton

[Printed by Gladstone at Oxford, 23 April 1831]

British Library, Add. MS 44721, folio 21, quoted in *The Prime Ministers' Papers Series: W.E. Gladstone, I. Autobiographica*, op. cit., p 230

Questions

a By what devices of style, and by what arguments, does

Gladstone denigrate his youthful political opinions? In what ways does he justify them?

★ *b* What was the wider international context of Gladstone's handbill (extract *b*)?

c To what extent does Gladstone belie his Canningite sympathies in the comments he makes on foreign affairs?

d If Gladstone's handbill echoes contemporary jargon, in what phrase or phrases does it foreshadow the Tamworth Manifesto?

e What support do you find in these extracts for the idea that the 1832 Reform Act deserves the title 'Great' in the eyes of advocates and opponents for having broken new ground?

5 'What is Mr. D'Israeli?'

(a) The charges

A letter to the Electors of Taunton [29 May 1835]

. . . What is Mr. D'Israeli? What are his claims to your support and confidence?

He is a young man, the son of a Jew, a stranger to the Town; known in the political world only by his inconsistency and his utter want of political principle. (5)

He claims your confidence because he is the author of three novels and a bad epic poem and because he can make a satirical and abusive speech.

(10) . . . But we are required to choose, not the best novelist, but the best politician; not the most fluent speaker, but the man of the most sound principles, not the most imaginative, but the most right judging man; not him who can abuse best, but him who knows most of political economy; not the greatest poet, but the best man of business. (15)

. . . He stands convicted of the grossest inconsistency. In 1833 he professed and advocated *Radical* opinions. In that year he offered himself as a candidate for the Borough of Mary-la-bone [Error: High Wycombe, not Marylebone], and he wrote a pamphlet under the title of '*What is he?*' In this pamphlet he avows himself a (20) Radical. In proof of this, and as if he had some doubt whether he would be believed, he states the measures he advocates. These are his words. 'What then, are the easiest and most obvious methods by which the DEMOCRATIC PRINCIPLE may be made predominant? It would appear that the easiest and most obvious (25) methods are the instant repeat of the Septennial Act, the institution of Election by Ballot, and the immediate dissolution of Parliament.' Such was his language only a very short time ago. Here can be *no mistake*! no sophistry can explain away *the fact* that in 1833 he advocated *ultra-radical* doctrines. He has himself stated in the same (30)

pamphlet that this was not a hasty but a deliberate judgment. 'I record here', he says, 'my *solemn conviction* and the result of my own *unprejudiced meditation*!' Moreover he asked and obtained of Mr. O'Connell, a letter of recommendation to the Electors of High
35 Wycombe. Will it be believed that he would have asked and received this favour, if he had not represented himself to that gentleman as a Radical? Add to this that he became a member of the Westminster Club, which was a Club formed by the Radical Party in the House of Commons to counteract the efforts of the
40 Conservative Club. . . .

Mr. D'Israeli's friends have confidently asserted that he is a man of fortune and rank, and that the expenses of the election are paid out of his own revenues. Now it so happens that one of the Solicitors of this Town was *in the same Office* with Mr. D'Israeli's
45 brother who was also a *Clerk* there. He is by this time I believe an Attorney. Now on the authority of that brother it appears that the Tory candidate's sole *property* consists of about £200 per annum, which his father allows him. . .

But what shall we say to his repeated assertions that he was not
50 assisted by the Conservative Club? He has no money of his own. Whose then does he spend? Or does he want to get into the house of Commons as a protection against *importunate friends?*

The Tories used to talk very loudly about the necessity of rank, character, and fortune distinguishing those whom we should
55 choose as representatives. Is it *thus* they illustrate their doctrines?

Somerset Record Office, DD/X/STT IC/239, pp 1–3, 12

(b) The answers

To the Electors and Inhabitants of the Borough of Taunton

I have just received a placard purporting to be a letter addressed to three respectable members of your community by an anonymous 'compiler', as he modestly styles himself, of a pamphlet
60 entitled, 'What is Mr. D'Israeli?'

This pamphlet was shown to me when I last had the honour of visiting Taunton, and I made no observation upon it for two reasons: firstly, because it was anonymous; and secondly, because it was absurd: every charge which it attempted to adduce having
65 already been confuted by me upon the hustings of your Borough and, in the estimation of all impartial persons, satisfactorily disposed of.

I have not his pamphlet by me, and I have only a vague recollection of some malicious observations expressed in a remark-
70 ably feeble style, but this anonymous Compiler who seems quite in a flutter that no one will reply to his lucubrations, favours us in his broadside with a '*summary*' of his charges, and to his own summary, as some of my friends seem to wish it, I now respond.

There are four accusations.

75 Firstly I am accused of gross political apostacy and inconsistency proved by my electioneering addresses and a certain pamphlet.

I have already given the reasons which induced me at one point to advocate the adoption of certain measures which are now I conceive unnecessary. I considered then that the adoption of those 80 measures could alone effect the formation of a national Party in the house of Commons which might keep the anti-national government in check, but the blunders of that government and the good sense of Englishmen have already, though unexpectedly produced that national Party, and therefore there is no necessity to have 85 recourse to political experiments to secure a benefit already obtained. . . .

Charge the 2nd. Ingratitude to Mr. O'Connell proved by the speech of that gentleman and the letter of Mr. Ronayne . . . [Disraeli refutes this charge by reference to his own attempts at 90 civility to O'Connell. The third charge, and Disraeli's reply, concern the challenge by Disraeli to Daniel O'Connell's son Morgan.]

The fourth charge has long ago been blown to the winds. My adversaries by a trick attempted to prove that I belonged to a 95 Radical Club. They accused me of belonging to the Westminster REFORM Club. *There is no such club in existence*; and I exposed the fruitless malice that attempts to convert a club formed avowedly for social purposes into a political confederacy. . . .

Whatever may be the fate of my political struggles in your 100 Borough, I can never forget the kindness and hospitality which I have experienced under your roofs; I must always feel that as a body, whatever may be your opinions, you are entitled to and possess my respect; and that for many of your members individually, I entertain a sincere regard and affection. Nevertheless 105 permit me to observe and believe me I make the observation without any affectation that my time is far too precious to waste it often in replying to such attacks as those of your Pamphleteer. . . .

I venture to add that no member of your Community will ever have cause to regret the confidence he has reposed in one who has 110 the honour to remain

With great respect and regard,
Your obliged and faithful servant,
BENJAMIN DISRAELI

London June 13th 1835

Somerset Record Office. DD/X/STT I C/239, pp. 1–7

Questions

a Of what value are these two extracts as evidence of electioneering tactics in the 1830s?

b What personal, as distinct from political, disqualifications does extract *a* argue in Disraeli's case?
c Identify the 'national party' and the 'anti-national party' (lines 80 and 81).
d What other materials would you wish to study to test the conflicting claims made in these two extracts?
e Do these extracts support the view that Disraeli was inconsistent in his early political opinions?

6 Disraeli on the hustings

B. D'ISRAELI, Esq. advanced to address the Electors, who received him with vehement cheers. He observed that the Whigs claimed great gratitude for having given the Reform Bill; he felt himself entitled to some portion of that sentiment for giving the
5 Electors of Taunton the first poll under it. . . . Whatever might be the result of the present proceedings, and he could not entertain any, he trusted that he should not leave a single enemy behind him, and if he were to be beaten any where, he did not know a place where defeat would be attended with so much alleviation as in
10 Taunton. From all persons, whether they agreed with him or not, he had experienced the most polite and hospitable reception. Mr. D'I. then adverted to an unfortunate expression he had used as to Mr. Labouchere's [the Whig candidate and minister's] having advanced to grasp the bloody hand of the traitor, O'Connell. He
15 never thought that this would have been literally contemplated. He had used the phrase figuratively, and meant nothing more than to deprecate the unhallowed alliance with the Irish demagogue, the consequences of which must be destructive. The measures in progress for appeasing Ireland were of unsound and mischievous
20 tendency, and the difficulty in the collection of tithes was not greater than 20 years ago was felt in England in the collection of rents ('How do you know that?' interposed one of the electors. 'Because', said Mr. D'Israeli, 'I have read, and you have not') (Laughter and applause)

The Taunton Courier and Western Advertiser, 24 April 1835

Questions

★ *a* With reference to this extract, to section 5 and your wider studies, describe the course of relations between Disraeli and Daniel O'Connell in 1834 and 1835. Do their relations inform us about the political direction in which Disraeli was moving at the time?
b What attitude does Disraeli show here towards Reform?
★ *c* What characteristics and traits of Disraeli's political style are displayed here?

II Peel's Second Ministry 1841–6

The 'hungry forties' appear as years of crisis. This is essentially a correct impression, and it is reinforced by the attention historians have always given to the articulate contemporary critics of Government – Shaftesbury and Disraeli, the Anti-Corn Law League and the Chartists – and to other social commentators such as Engels and Dickens.

It would be reasonable to expect, then, that a critical view of Peel would have triumphed. Weaknesses in his political style, his alienation of the grass roots of the Tory party and the fall of his government in 1846 would be highlighted. Instead, he has generally enjoyed a good press, from his contemporary Guizot to his eminent modern biographer Norman Gash. He is represented as a successful economic and social reformer, and the self-sacrificing man of the hour in 1846. His early death, and the fact that his advocates, such as Queen Victoria and Gladstone, tended to outlive his detractors, may partly account for this reputation.

To test the relative merits of these two views of Peel and his Government, some questions should be asked. Who deserves credit for the gradual relief of working and living conditions in Britain? If the free trade movement, to which Peel's policies made a large contribution, set the seal on Britain's position as the 'workshop of the world', did they not also prepare a favourable environment for Britain's agricultural and industrial competitors in the second half of the century? Did Peel's Government have a foreign policy as recognisable as that of, say, Canning or Palmerston? Could Peel have done more to anticipate or relieve the disaster in Ireland? Did the repeal of the Corn Laws help materially at all?

Lord John Russell's biographer, John Prest, has performed the valuable task of drawing attention to Peel's opposite number. Russell's behaviour in 1845, his failure to take the 'poisoned chalice' following his conversion to repeal, deserves scrutiny, not least for its influence on Peel's actions in 1846.

1 The View from across the Channel

[Original in French]

He arrived in power under the most brilliant and yet the most precarious auspices, with dazzling strengths and also with hidden weaknesses. His triumph was as legitimate as it was complete: the

Whig cabinet had succumbed to no accident, no manoeuvre; it was
5 slowly worn down, in the full light of serious debate, and retreated before the positive and deliberate vote of parliament. The cabinet which Peel had just formed counted in its breast the most renowned men in glory, in rank, in ability and in esteem: in the chamber of Peers, the Duke of Wellington, without portfolio; Lord
10 Lyndhurst, as skilful in political discussions as in the administration of justice; Lord Aberdeen, concilliatory as well as noble in spirit, prudent, patient, fair-minded, and better informed than anyone concerning the diplomatic interests and traditions of Europe; Lord Ellenborough, the most brilliant tory orator; – in the Commons
15 chamber, Lord Stanley, whom the noble former chief of the Whigs, Lord Grey, regarded, as he told me in 1840, as the most direct heir of the great oratorical school of Pitt and Fox; Sir James Graham, the eminent administrator, prolific and animated polemicist, resourceful in debates; – around him, a group of men still
20 young and already very distinguished, hard-working, enlightened, committed, devoted; Mr. Gladstone, Lord Lincoln, Mr. Sidney Herbert, Sir William Follett. . . .

But he was called to the most difficult of tasks, to an essentially incoherent and contradictory task. He was obliged to be at the same
25 time a conservative and a reformer, and to carry with him, in this twofold path, a majority incoherent in itself and in which, at the core, sectional interests, prejudices and immovable and intractable passions dominated. . . .

His situation and his mission were equally complex and
30 encumbered; he was a *bourgeois* with the task of causing a powerful and proud aristocracy to submit to tough reforms, a sensible and moderate liberal, but a liberal all the same, dragging in his train the old tories and the ultra-protestants. . . .

Francois Guizot, *Sir Robert Peel, Etude d'Histoire Contemporaire,* Paris 1856, pp 82–4

Questions

a What were Guizot's credentials for commentating on Peel's ministry? At what point does he claim the most direct evidence?

b Can you account for Lord Grey's compliment to Lord Stanley?

★ *c* How sound is Guizot's assessment of the strengths and weaknesses of Peel's position in 1841?

2 Free trade

(a) Peel adjusts the Corn Law

Cabinet Memorandum: Winter of 1841

The first question for the Cabinet to determine in reference to the subject of the Corn Laws is, whether they will, as a Cabinet,

undertake the consideration of those laws, and propose to Parliament a legislative measure re-adjusting the duties which
5 regulate the import of foreign corn.

I shall assume in this Paper that, if there is to be a re-adjustment of those duties, the principle of the present law, that is, a scale of duty varying inversely with the price of corn in the home market, is to be adopted in preference to a fixed duty.

10 I apprehend that there are few persons who would maintain that the present scale of duties is perfect, and admits of no amendment – that of those who think the protection it ensures to home produce is not, upon the whole, too great, the great majority would feel that the mode in which the protection is afforded is defective; and that,
15 on account of the rapid and sudden diminution of the duties when the price of corn is rising above 67s [shillings per quarter, i.e. £2.85 per approx 13 kilos], there are great temptations to tampering with the averages; that there is great risk, in consequence, of unnecessary loss to the revenue, and of injury, at certain seasons and under
20 certain circumstances, to domestic agriculture, from the sudden admission into home consumption of a considerable and needless quantity of foreign corn at a low rate of duty. . . .

The population of Great Britain was, in

1821 14,071,000
25 1831 16,263,000
1841 18,531,000

Up to the year 1773 this country exported wheat.

It is stated in the Report of the Agricultural Committee of 1821 that from the year 1695 to the year 1773 the excess of exports over
30 imports of grain was 31 million of quarters. Since the commencement of the operation of the present Corn Law, that is since July 1828, there have been admitted into home consumption 11,271,000 quarters of foreign wheat, and 3,724,000 cwt [hundredweight, i.e. approx 50 kilos] of foreign wheat flour. . . .
35 [Peel proposes an elongation of the sliding scale]

By these means I gain three advantages:

First. Benefit to the revenue

Secondly. Benefit to the consumer, by giving him access to an increased supply when the price arrives at such a point as 65s or 66s
40 [£2.75 or £2.80].

Thirdly. Benefit to the farmer, by preventing a sudden and great influx of corn at a nominal duty.

Memoirs of Sir Robert Peel, ed. Lord Mahon and Edward Cardwell, Parts II and III, 1857, pp 327–8, 331–2, 356

(b) First blood in the Corn Law battle

To Lord de Grey February 7 1842

There is not one word of truth about Knatchbull [rumoured to be

45 hostile to the Corn Law amendments]. He is entirely satisfied, and in the Cabinet the Duke of Buckingham has no adherents. Even in the Carlton Club I don't think he has many, though, of course, there are some *frondeurs* [rebels, by analogy with seventeenth-century France] and some alarmists.

50 The Duke of Buccleuch's prompt acceptance, on a full knowledge of our measures, has blunted the edge of the cut from the Duke of Buckingham, and his acceptance of the Blue Ribbon on retiring has diminished his powers of opposition, even if he were disposed to exercise it in the spirit of hostility, which at present is 55 by no means the case.

We shall succeed with our corn; our great difficulties will be taxation and finance.

February 10 – Our Corn Law proposition has succeeded as well as I could have hoped. To our opponents nothing that we could 60 with honesty propose would be satisfactory. Our aim was to meet the reasonable expectations of moderate men, without offending or injuring the landed interests. I am disposed to hope that we have succeeded in our object, and that we shall keep the main body of our party together.

65 The real trial still remains, and this will be the demand of an increase of income by fresh taxes.

I know not whether Parliament and the country will sustain us in the decisive policy which we must recommend.

March 8 – On Friday Peel will open his plan of finance; and I 70 conceive this to be the cardinal point on which our fortunes turn. If his proposed measures be accepted by the country, we are irresistible; if they be rejected, power has departed from us.

March 16 – Our financial measures may be considered safe. In the main the public, has adopted them, and the position of the 75 Government is secured.

C.S. Parker, *Life and Letters of Sir James Graham*, Vol. I, 1907, pp 316–7

(c) Tariffs and income tax

In August 1842, Sir Robert having taken office, found a deficiency of two-and-a-half millions, occasioned by three nearly simultaneous wars waged in Syria, China, and Affghanistan [*sic*]. He remarked therefore rightly, that the imposition of the income tax 80 was 'not a mere gratuitous act but a measure rendered absolutely necessary by the circumstances of the case'. . . . He also justified it by the fact that recently imposed indirect taxes had been carried to the uttermost and without producing an equivalent revenue. . . .

Among the great benefits of direct taxation is its far greater 85 economy in three ways. In the first place the people would save half the whole amount now spent on the levy of Customs and Excise –

supposing customs to be altogether abolished – therefore by this amount would taxation be decreased. But there would be another and far larger gain, not always borne in mind. The consumers of
90 indirectly taxed articles pay much more in addition to the value of the article than the actual duty, the price of the goods being always augmented by more than the tax. Mr. J.S. Mill, the eminent economist, admits this.

There is a third advantage, and that is the diminution, if not
95 removal, of the present irresistible inducement to adulterate taxed goods which the duties create. . . . The import and excise duties on articles of food are the great cause of this pernicious and abominable destruction of health and life, and this is a strong reason for their abolition. . . .

100 To the all-important interest of the working man in his scheme of an income tax, Sir Robert Peel showed that he was fully alive. He said in one of his speeches – '. . . I do think myself warranted in saying that I have done all that could be accomplished for the working man; and most especially do I say this. When I remember
101 that I have exempted from the tax all incomes below £150 a year. . . . April 8, 1842.'

Jelinger Symons, *Sir Robert Peel, As a Type of Statesmanship*, 1856, pp 128–9, 131, 139

Questions

- *a* Does Peel set about reforming the Corn Laws from a position of principle or on practical grounds? Use extract *a* to support your opinion.
- *b* Who were the opponents of the 1842 Corn Law amendment (see extract *b*)?
- *c* What character traits of Sir James Graham are revealed by extract *b*?
- *d* What questionable assumptions about the benefits of free trade does the author of extract *c* make?
- *e* Taken as a whole, were Peel's tax and tariff changes beneficial to 'the working man' (extract *c*, line 100)?
- ★ *f* What were the precedents for tariff reductions, and what was the subsequent progress of free trade?

3 Mines and Factories

(a) The Mines Bill – Shaftesbury triumphant

May 7th [1842] – The report of the Commission [on mines] is out – a noble document. The Home Office in vain endeavoured to hold it back: it came by a most providential mistake into the hands of members; and though the Secretary of State for a long while

5 prevented the sale of it, he could not prevent publicity, or any notice of motion.

Perhaps even 'Civilization' itself never exhibited such a mass of sin and cruelty. The disgust felt is very great, thank God; but will it be reduced to action when I call for a remedy?

10 May 14th – The Government cannot, if they would, refuse the Bill of which I have given notice, to exclude females and children from coal-pits – the feeling in my favour has become quite enthusiastic; the Press on all sides is working most vigorously. . . .

May 24th – One would have thought that a 'paternal' Government 15 would have hastened to originate, certainly to aid, any measures for the removal of this foul and cruel stain? No such thing, no assistance, no sympathy – every obstacle in my way, though I doubt whether they will dare openly to *oppose* me on the Bill itself. Have no time for reflection, no time for an entry. I hear that no 20 such sensation has been caused since the first disclosures of the horrors of the slave trade! God, go before us, as in Thy pillar of a cloud!

June 1st. . . . I foresee a covert and spiteful opposition; the Great Northern coal-owners have produced a document of defence of 25 themselves, which throws the mantle of their comparative merit over the enormities of the general practice. Here is party! It is a vain, insolent, and feeble paper, quite in the style of the old apologies of the Factory masters. . . .

June 9th – Oh that I had the tongue of an angel to express what I 30 ought to feel! God grant that I may never forget it, for I cannot record it. On the 7th, brought forward my motion – the success has been *wonderful*, yes, really wonderful – for two hours the House listened so attentively that you might have heard a pin drop, broken only by loud and repeated marks of approbation. . . .

35 June 16th – Accounts from all parts full of promise. The collier people themselves are delighted; the hand-loom weavers (poor people!) rejoice in the exclusion of the females, as they themselves will go down and take their places. . . .

July 8th – Much, very much trouble to find a peer who would take 40 charge of the Bill. It is 'the admiration of every body, but the choice of none'. . . . All had some excuse or other; praised it, but avoided it. . . . [The Bill passes the Lords].

August 8th – Took the Sacrament on Sunday in joyful and humble thankfulness to Almighty God for the undeserved measure of 45 success with which he has blessed my effort for the glory of His name, and the welfare of His creatures. . . .

Edwin Hodder, *The Life and Work of the Seventh Earl of Shaftesbury*, Vol. I, 1887, pp 418–21, 426, 429, 431

(b) The Factory Bill

On the 5th of February, Sir James Graham introduced in the House of Commons, a Bill for the regulation of labour in factories, which the Government had prepared to submit to Parliament. The educational clauses in the measure of the preceding year which had occasioned such warm controversy were not included in the present Bill. Sir James Graham briefly explained the proposed enactments. With respect to the age, he proposed that the term 'child' should be defined to mean children between nine and thirteen, instead of eight and thirteen; that such children should not be employed for a longer time than six and a half hours each day: and that they should not be employed in the forenoon and the afternoon of the same day. In the existing [1833] law 'young persons' were defined to be persons between the ages of thirteen and eighteen: he did not propose any alteration in that part of the Act, but he should propose that such 'young persons' should not be employed in any silk, cotton, wool or flax manufactory, for any portion of the twenty-four hours longer than from half-past five o'clock to seven o'clock in the summer, and half-past six o'clock to eight o'clock in the winter; thus making thirteen hours and a half each day, of which one hour and a half should be allowed for meals and rest. In respect to females, they should not under any circumstances be required to work more than twelve hours out of the twenty-four. . . .

Annual Register, 1844, pp 107–8

(c) Shaftesbury forced to compromise

May 14th [1844] – Last night defeated – utterly, singularly, prodigiously defeated by a majority of 138!! The House seemed aghast, perplexed, astounded. No one could say how, why and almost when. It seemed that 35 or 40 was the highest majority expected. Such is the power and such the exercise of ministerial influence!. . . .

May 15th – The majority was one to save the Government (even the Whigs being reluctant to turn them out just now), not against the question of Ten Hours. . . .

May 16th – Dined last night at the Lord Mayor's feast. Found much sympathy, as I do everywhere. . . . Peel and Graham tried to make fair weather with me afterwards. Did not rebuff them, though I could not *feel* either friendship or esteem. . . . Amply satisfied now that I permitted the withdrawal of the Bill. Should have been defeated by an equal majority, and the question would have been ended for the Session. But what should I have lost? The interval has produced all these public meetings, all the witnesses they exhibited, all the feeling they roused, not only throughout those provinces, but the whole country, and, finally, I have obtained a debate and division on the true issue of the *Ten Hours*, not on a mere technicality. Have I not, moreover, saved the Bill with all its valuable clauses about machinery and female labour?. . . . [The Bill became law on 6th June 1844].

Edwin Hodder, *The Life and Work of the Seventh Earl of Shaftesbury,* Vol. II, 1887, p 50

Questions

★ *a* What, in general terms, was the 'mass of sin and cruelty revealed in 1842' (extract *a*, lines 7–8)?

b From the internal evidence of extract *a*, is Shaftesbury justified in accusing the Government of delaying and obstructing the bill?

c What arguments were being raised against the evidence of the Mines Commission?

d By comparing extract *b* and *c*, suggest the viewpoint of the Annual Register in the matter of the Factory Bill?

e Why had 'educational clauses . . . occasioned such warm controversy' (extract *b*, lines 50–51)?

f Comment on Shaftesbury's tactics over the Factory Bill, and their degree of success.

g By reference to the details of extracts *b* and *c*, say whether the 1844 Factory Act gave any protection to adult men.

★ *h* In his own terms, what were Shaftesbury's motives for campaigning for reform of working conditions? What did his detractors say? What range of motives did other reformers have?

4 Foreign Affairs – Tahiti in particular

It is by no means improbable that the acquisition of [the Marquesas Islands] may prove to the French another Algeria on a smaller scale – an *Algerietta*. They have, in fact, already, it seems, given a new and most discriminating name to a group, which is henceforth to
5 be called the 'Oceanic Islands', as if there were no islands in other oceans. Does the old name of Pacific not square exactly with their views of what may happen, or be intended?. . . .

Lord Lansdowne is putting a question, in the House of Lords, regarding the alleged occupation of, as the protection to be given
10 by the King of the French to, the island of Tahiti, observed 'that for a number of years past, a very great improvement in the civilization and religious instruction of the inhabitants of Tahiti, and its other islands, amounting, he believed, to a population of 150,000 souls, had taken place, that this had been occasioned by persons who,
15 from beneficent and religious motives, had taken up their residence there, and by their influence had induced the inhabitants entirely to change the habits of life – to introduce education and to found

schools, which are now numerous. He wished, therefore, to know, if the government had received such explanations and assurances
20 that English settlers in Tahiti would obtain from the French authorities that degree of protection which was justly their due; – that they would not be subject to any unjust treatment, or above all things, to expulsion from these islands.'

Lord Aberdeen, in reply, states, that 'he was not sufficiently
25 informed of the precise grounds upon which the French government had acted, or of complaints made against the authorities in those islands, which had led to the convention; but he had no apprehension as to the establishment of the French in those seas, nor that our commercial or political interests would be affected by it.'

Edinburgh Review, Vol. 79, 1844, p 49–50

Questions

★ *a* Which events brought Anglo-French relations over Tahiti to a head?

b Does the tone of this article reveal its bias?

★ *c* Was there a well-founded Anglo-French entente during Peel's term of office, or could Aberdeen be accused of complacency?

5 Maynooth

April 6th 1845

Everybody is telling of the great stir that is making in the country against the Maynooth grant and the large increase to Peel's unpopularity which it has produced. Some even fancy that he will have difficulty in carrying the measure through, but I incline to
5 think the difficulty indoors and the excitement without are both overrated, and certainly will not be enough to arrest the progress of the measure; but that it disgusts the Tory party and creates fresh sources of dislike and discussion between the great body of the Conservatives and the Government is indubitable, and Peel and his
10 colleagues are so well aware of this, that they think something must, before long, occur to break up the Government. . . .

The truth is that the Government is Peel, that Peel is a reformer and more of a Whig than a Tory, and that the mass of his followers are prejudiced, ignorant, obstinate and selfish. In his speech the
15 other night he certainly said nothing calculated to coax or soothe his angry people, and still less did he utter a word about finality, or give out that this was to be the limit of concession. . . .

The Greville Memoirs, ed. Henry Reeve, Vol. V, 1888, pp 283–4

Questions

★ *a* Why did Peel increase the grant to Maynooth College? Why did Gladstone resign over the issue? Was his opposition to the grant characteristic of Tory opposition to the measure?

★ *b* Do you agree with Greville that the breakup of Peel's Government and party was likely to take place even without the Corn Law crisis of 1845–6?

6 The crisis breaks

(a) *Graham considers the options*

Sir J. Graham to Sir R. Peel — Netherby [near Carlisle] October 13 [1845]

. . . The time has now arrived when the potatoes are taken out of the ground, and when speculation on the subject is reduced to certainty. A great national risk is always incurred when a population so dense as that of Ireland subsists on the potato; for it is 5 the cheapest and the lowest food, and if it fails, no substitute can be found for starving multitudes.

It will be necessary after this warning that we should apply our immediate thoughts and attention to measures which may mitigate this national calamity; for human skill can supply no remedy.

10 In Belgium and in Holland, if I mistake not, a similar evil has been met by opening the ports to all articles of first necessity for human food. It is desirable that we should know, without loss of time, what has been done by our Continental neighbours in similar circumstances. Indian corn [maize] might be obtained from the 15 United States readily, and on cheap terms, if the people would eat it; but unfortunately it is an acquired taste; and if we opened the ports to maize duty-free, most popular and irresistible arguments present themselves why flour and oatmeal, the staple of the food of man, should not be restricted in its supply by artificial means, while 20 Heaven has withheld from an entire people its accustomed sustenance. Could we with propriety remit duties in November by Order in Council, when Parliament might so easily be called together? Can these duties, once remitted by Act of Parliament, be ever again reimposed? Ought they to be maintained with their 25 present stringency, if the people of Ireland be reduced to the last extremity for want of food?

Memoirs of Sir Robert Peel, ed. Lord Mahon and Edward Cardwell, Parts II and III, 1857, pp 114–15

(b) *Russell refuses the poisoned chalice*

Chesham Place: December 20, 1845

Lord John Russell presents his humble duty to your Majesty, and has the honour to state that he has found it impossible to form an Administration.

30 Lord John Russell was aware, from the first moment when your Majesty was pleased to propose to him this commission, that there were very great difficulties in the way, which it required the most cordial co-operation on the part of his friends, and the firm support of a large portion of those who followed Sir Robert Peel, to 35 surmount.

Lord John Russell has had solely in view the settlement of the question of the Corn Laws by which the country is so much agitated. . . .

Lord John Russell is quite ready to admit that Sir Robert Peel has 40 been willing from the commencement to the end to diminish the difficulties in the course of a new Government prepared to attempt the settlement of the Corn Laws. But Sir Robert Peel could not, of course, rely on the support of his political friends should the proposed measure be in their eyes dangerous or otherwise. . . .

Spencer Walpole, *The Life of Lord John Russell*, Vol. I, 1889, pp 417–18

Questions

★ *a* Why had the people of rural Ireland become so dependent on the potato crop?

b Explain, with support from extract *a*, why Graham saw no alternative to total repeal of the Corn Laws.

c Was repeal a sufficient measure? What other active measures were considered or carried out?

d Do Lord John Russell's explanations (extract *b*) sufficiently account for his inability to form a government?

★ *e* Did Russell's attempt and failure to form a government strengthen or weaken Peel's hand in 1846?

7 For and Against the Corn Laws

(a) The League

A meeting of the League was held in the free Trade Hall on the 28th of October [1845]. The object of the meeting was to point out the remedy for the famine which threatened England, and to avert the misery, starvation, and death of millions in Ireland. Mr. Cobden 5 said the natural and obvious remedy was to open the ports. Russia, Turkey, Germany and Holland had done so, and why should not our Government follow their example? Mr. Bright said that everything around was telling them in a voice louder than ever that every word of reproach, every harsh saying which they had uttered 10 against the Corn Laws, had not by any means conveyed its true

character as it was then exhibited. The Corn Law was now having its due effect, and one which its farmers anticipated – that of taking something from the produce of the millions of almost starving poor, and handing it to the rich. Looking at the matter in every
15 light, he added, 'How dreadful the abandonment of duty, how awful the crime, not less than that of those who made the Corn Law, if we step back from our place, if we fail in the work we have set ourselves, which is to abolish the law that restricts the bounty of Providence, and to establish the original and heaven – given law
20 which will give plenty to all the earth.'

George Barnett Smith, *The Life and Speeches of the Right Hon. John Bright*, M.P., Vol. I, 1881, p 206

(b) A Protectionist argument

[20 Feb. 1846]

DISRAELI: We have thrown upon the land the revenues of the Church, the administration of justice, and the estate of the poor; and you value that territorial constitution, not as serving to gratify the pride or pamper the luxury of the proprietors of the land, but
25 because in a territorial Constitution, you, and those whom you have succeeded, have found the only security for self-government; the only barrier against that centralising system which has taken root in other countries.

I know that we have been told, and by one [Cobden] who on this
30 subject should be the highest authority, that we shall derive from this great struggle, not merely the repeal of the Corn Laws, but the transfer of power from one class to another – to one distinguished for its intelligence and wealth, the manufacturers of England. My conscience assures me that I have not been slow in doing justice to
35 the intelligence of that class; certain I am, that I am not one of those who envy them their wide and deserved prosperity; but I must confess my deep mortification, that in an age of political regeneration, when all social evils are ascribed to the operation of class interests, it should be suggested that we are to be rescued from the
40 alleged power of one class only to sink under the avowed dominion of another. . . .

Hansard, 3rd Series, Vol. 83, 1846, Columns 1346–7

Questions

a Identify the League, and the venue of its meeting (extract *a*, line 1).

b Does Disraeli (extract *b*) adduce any economic arguments in defence of the Corn Laws?

c Use extracts *a* and *b* to show in what ways the argument about the Corn Laws was a clash of interests and classes. Were there any common interests in the matter?

8 Retrospective

To Sir Robert Peel

Netherby [near Carlisle]
September 4, 1846

The farmers in this neighbourhood will not venture again to plant potatoes on a large scale, and the poor are gladly resorting to the use of Indian meal and of bread compounded of Indian meal and American flour, which is cheap and nutritious.

5 I consider it the most fortunate event of my life to have been enabled in any degree, however slight, to contribute to the attainment of this national good, which compensates for a severe dispensation of Providence. And you will think of this and be comforted when friends forsake you, when enemies assail you, and
10 when the tinsel of the vanities of public life becomes tarnished in your estimation.

C.S. Parker, *Life and Letters of Sir James Graham*, Vol. II, 1907, p 52

Questions

a What light does this extract shed on the impact of the potato famine on England?

b Does 'a severe dispensation of providence' sufficiently account for the potato famine?

⋆ *c* Did the public estimation of Peel between 1846 and 1850 correspond to Graham's estimation?

III The Conservative Party from Peel to Disraeli

There is a historiographical tradition that associates the origin of the label 'Conservative' with the period of Peel's Tamworth Manifesto. The label is in fact a little older, but anyway the tradition is too neat. Peel was not setting an agenda for a modern political party. He was a ministerialist in the Pittite mould, who believed that the King's (or Queen's) government must be carried on. His Tamworth address, called a 'manifesto' by the liberal *Morning Chronicle*, contains no mention of the term 'conservative' – no reference, indeed, to 'party' by that name.

The creation of the Carlton Club, the work of the 1830s and the victory in 1841 mark a progression, but after 1846 the tories were a party in need of policies, in need of popular support and in need of a leader. Despite Derby's efforts and the brief periods of minority government, these deficiencies were not supplied until they came together, very improbably, in the person of Disraeli. To him, John Gorst and the new party organisations belong the credit for the 1874 election victory, which ushered in the only purely Conservative majority government between 1846 and 1922.

Disraeli, who had first presented as a radical, then become the champion of the protectionist backwoodsmen, reached his zenith as the tory populist if not the tory democrat.

The history of the Conservative party has been very coherently analysed by Robert Blake. More narrowly focused studies by H.J. Hanham and Paul Smith have enquired more deeply into the bases of party and election management and the phenomenon of a Conservative government of social reform.

Always the student must bear in mind that party links were looser than in the twentieth century. Can we confidently ascribe the changing fortunes of Tories and Liberals to their deliberate actions in the fields of domestic, Irish and foreign affairs, or were elections won and lost just as often on the vagaries of cross-voting, uncontested elections, local loyalties and the play of personalities?

1 The Hundred Days

(a) Grass roots

Wellingborough Conservatives
(From the *Northampton Herald*)

The proceedings of the Conservative Club established two years ago in the northern division of the county have from the first attracted great attention. The energy and spirit with which its proceedings have been conducted have helped, not to create good feelings, for they had been already created, but to preserve and ever increase the feelings of loyalty to the king, attachment to the principle of church and state, and a resolution to support the agricultural interest. The circumstances of the country and the dismissal of the Whig administration had caused, as may be easily imagined, an increased activity among the members of this Conservative Club. . . . The dinner took place in the large room of the Hind Inn, at Wellingborough, but at a later hour than had been fixed, in consequence of the unexpected number of arrivals from various parts of the neighbourhood. . . . The guests, whether as landlords or as tenants, may be said to have represented by far the largest part of the landed property in the vicinity of Wellingborough. . . . In Wellingborough, one of the most Radical towns in England three years ago, and always by far the most Radical town in Northamptonshire, the Conservatives were loudly cheered by the inhabitants assembled to see them arrive and depart. . . .

[After toasts] T.P. Maunsell, Esq., rose and said – Gentlemen . . . the dismissal of the late Ministry by his most gracious Majesty . . . has indeed thrown a ray of sunshine over the country which I most fervently hope may illuminate it for many years to come. I shall very briefly advert to the conduct of the ex-ministers while in office. The professed advocates of economy and the self-styled reformers of abuses, they created commission on commission, and place after place, which they bestowed with a most liberal hand upon their own relatives and friends. (Laughter). The professed advocates of the abolition of those taxes which pressed most heavily upon those least able to bear them, they repealed some, whose remission benefitted nobody, they repealed others (I allude particularly to the taxes upon coals and upon houses) which chiefly, I may say almost exclusively, benefitted the wealthy householders in London and in the great manufacturing towns, a very large majority of whom they knew to be their staunch supporters and friends. . . . They held out their new code of poor laws as a relief to that interest. It may, and I trust will, force the sturdy idle pauper to work; but I know too well the kind and humane dispositions of the occupiers of the soil to suppose for one moment that they would derive relief at the expense and by the oppression of the destitute and the aged. (Cheers) Under the government of the Whig Ministry the agricultural interest particularly suffered, their affairs proceeded from bad to worse, and had those Ministers continued in office a free trade in corn would have consummated their ruin (Cheers.). . . .

The Times, 3 Feb 1835

(b) The Tamworth Manifesto

50 TO THE ELECTORS
OF THE
BOROUGH OF TAMWORTH

GENTLEMEN

On 26th of November last, being at Rome, I received from his
55 Majesty a summons, wholly unforseen and expected by me, to return to England without delay, for the purpose of assisting his Majesty in the formation of a new Government. I instantly obeyed the command for my return, and, on my arrival, I did not hesitate, after an anxious review of the position of public affairs, to place at
60 the disposal of my Sovereign any services which I might be thought capable of rendering. . . .

The King, in a crisis of great difficulty, required my services. The question I had to decide was this: Shall I obey the call; or shall I shrink from the responsibility, alleging as the reason that I consider
65 myself, in consequence of the Reform Bill, as labouring under a sort of disqualification which must preclude me, and all who think with me, both now and for ever from entering into the official service of the Crown? Would it, I ask, be becoming in any public man to act upon such a principle? Was it fit that I should assume
70 that either the object or the effect of the Reform Bill has been to preclude all hope of a successful appeal to the good sense and calm judgment of the people, and so to flatter the prerogative of the Crown that the King has no free choice among his subjects, but must select his Ministers from one section, and one section only of
75 public men. . . .

Now, I say at once, that I will not accept power on the condition of declaring myself an apostate from the principles on which I have heretofore acted. At the same time I never will admit that I have been, either before or after the Reform Bill, the defender of abuses,
80 or the enemy of judicious reforms. I appeal with confidence, in denial of the charge, to the active part which I took in the great question of currency – in the consolidation and amendment of the criminal law – in the revisal of the whole system of Trial by Jury – to the opinions I have professed, and uniformly acted on with
85 regard to other branches of the jurisprudence of the country. . . .

With respect to the Reform Bill itself. I will repeat now the declaration which I made when I entered the House of Commons as a Member of the Reformed Parliament, that I consider the Reform Bill a final and irrevocable settlement of a great constitutio-
90 nal question – a settlement which no friend to the peace and welfare of this country would attempt to disturb, either by direct or by insidious means.

Then as to the spirit of the Reform Bill, and the willingness to adopt and enforce it as a rule of government. If by adopting the

95 spirit of the Reform Bill it be meant that we are to live in a perpetual vortex of agitation – that public men can only support themselves in public estimation by adopting every popular impression of the day, by promising the instant redress of anything which anybody may call an abuse . . . if this be the spirit of the
100 Reform Bill, I will not undertake to adopt it; but if the spirit of the Reform Bill implies merely a careful review of institutions, civil and ecclesiastical, undertaken in a friendly temper, combining, with the firm maintenance of established rights, the correction of proved abuses, and the redress of real grievances, in that case I can,
105 for myself and my colleagues, undertake to act in such a spirit, and with such intentions [Peel proceeds to outline certain policies in detail]. . . .

It is unnecessary for my purposes to enter into further details. I have said enough, with respect to general principles and their
110 practical application to public measures, to indicate the spirit in which the King's Government is prepared to act. Our object will be the maintenance of peace, the scrupulous and honourable fulfilment, without reference to their original policy, of all existing engagements with foreign Powers, the support of public credit, the
115 enforcement of strict economy, and the just and impartial consideration of what is due to all interests, agricultural, manufacturing, and commercial. . . .

I am, Gentlemen,
With affectionate regard,
120 Most faithfully yours,
(signed) ROBERT PEEL.

The Memoirs of Sir Robert Peel, ed. Lord Mahon and Edward Cardwell, Part I, 1857, pp 58–67

Questions

- ★ *a* In what circumstances were the Wellingborough Conservative Club and others like it founded?
- *b* What appears to be the political bias of the author of the *Northampton Herald* article reproduced in *The Times* (extract *a*)?
- ★ *c* What were the circumstances of the fall of the Whig Ministry in 1834? Why was Peel called for in preference to the Duke of Wellington, despite his absence from the country?
- ★ *d* To what extent did it appear by 1834 that the Whigs would 'live in a perpetual vortex of agitation' (extract *b*, lines 95–6)?
- *e* To what extent do Maunsell's and Peel's agendas for the Conservative Party coincide and to what extent do they differ?
- ★ *f* Does the Tamworth Manifesto deserve to be regarded as a foundation of Conservative theory?

2 Peel in opposition

February 18th 1838

I know no more of Peel's opinions and designs than what I can gather from his conduct and what he is likely to entertain under present circumstances; but it must be his object to delay coming 5 into office till he can do so as a powerful Minister, and till it is made manifest to Parliament and the Country that he is demanded by a great public exigency, and is not marching in as the result of a party triumph. If the resignation of the present Government should take place under any circumstances which admitted of a reunion of the 10 Whigs and Radicals, and of the whole reunited party being held together in opposition to a Conservative Government, Peel would be little more secure, and not more able to act with efficiency and independence than he was in 1835, and this is what he will never submit to. . . .

15 His interest therefore (and consequently I suppose his design) is to restrain the impatience of his followers; to let the Government lose ground in public estimation gently and considerately, not violently and rancorously: to assist in putting them in a contemptible or inefficient point of view; to render their places, so that his 20 return to power may be more in appearance the art of the Whig Ministry than any act of his own.

The Greville Memoirs, ed. Henry Reeve, Vol. IV, 1888, pp 64–5

Questions

★ *a* Did the events of 1839 confirm Greville's predictions about the conditions on which Peel would accept office?

★ *b* Does this extract support the proposition that Disraeli 'invented' the idea of a vigorous and active opposition in the 1870s?

3 Disraeli's critique of Peel

(a) In the heat of the moment

[15 May 1846]

[Disraeli:] Sir, this country can only exist by free discussion. If it is once supposed that opinions are to be put down by any other means, then, whatever may be our political forms, liberty vanishes. If we think the opinions of the Anti-Corn-Law League are 5 dangerous – if we think their system is founded on error, and must lead to confusion – it is open in a free country like England for men who hold opposite ideas to resist them with the same earnestness, by all legitimate means – by the same active organization, and by all the intellectual power they command. But what happens in this

10 country? A body of gentlemen, able and adroit men, come forward, and profess contrary doctrines to those of these new economists. They place themselves at the head of that great popular party who are adverse to the new ideas, and, professing their opinions, they climb and clamber into power by having accepted,
15 or rather by having eagerly sought the trust. It follows that the body whom they represent, trusting in their leaders, not unnaturally slumber at their posts. They conclude that their opinions are represented in the State. . . . Well, Sir, what happens? The right hon. Gentleman, the First Minister, told his friends that he had
20 given them very significant hints of the change of his opinions. . . . I remember, when the Whig budget was rejected, and the right hon. Gentleman was installed into office, the changes which he proposed at the time created some suspicion: but all suspicion was hushed at the moment, because the right hon. Gentleman was
25 looked upon as the man who could make the 'best bargain' for the party. I want to know what Gentlemen think of their best bargain now?

. . . I have that confidence in the common sense, I will say the common spirit of our countrymen, that I believe they will not long
30 endure this huckstering tyranny of the Treasury Bench – these political pedlars that bought their party in the cheapest market, and sold us in the dearest. I know, Sir, that there are many who believe that the time is gone by when one can appeal to those high and honest impulses that were once the mainstay and the main element
35 of the English character. I know, Sir, that we appeal to a people debauched by public gambling – stimulated and encouraged by an inefficient and shortsighted Minister. I know that the public mind is polluted with economic fancies: a depraved desire that the rich may become richer without the interference of industry and toil. I
40 know, Sir, that all confidence in public men is lost. But, Sir, I have faith in the primitive and enduring elements of the English Character. . . . But the dark and inevitable hour will arrive. Then, when their spirit is softened by misfortune, they will recur to those principles that made England great, and which, in our belief, can
45 alone keep England great. Then, too, perchance, they may remember, not with unkindness, those who betrayed and deserted, were neither ashamed nor afraid to struggle for the 'good old cause' – the cause with which are associated principles the most popular, sentiments the most entirely national – the cause of labour – the
50 cause of the people – the cause of England.

[Peel]: Sir, I believe it is now nearly three months since I first proposed, as the organ of Her Majesty's Government, the measure which, I trust, is about to receive to-night the sanction of the House of Commons; and, considering the lapse of time – considering the
55 frequent discussions – considering the anxiety of the people of this

country that these debates should be brought to a close, I feel that I should be offering an insult to the House – I should be offering an insult to the country – if I were to condescend to bandy personalities upon such an occasion. Sir, I foresaw that the course which I have taken from a sense of public duty would expose me to
60 serious sacrifices. I foresaw as its inevitable result that I must forfeit friendships which I most highly valued – that I must interrupt political relations in which I felt a sincere pride; but the smallest of all penalties which I anticipated were the continued venomous attacks of the Member for Shrewsbury [Peel and Disraeli proceed
65 to disagree as to whether Disraeli had sought office under Peel in 1841].

Hansard, 3rd Series, Vol. 86, 1846, columns 672–677, 689

(b) In retrospect

Nature had combined in Sir Robert Peel many admirable parts. In him a physical frame incapable of fatigue was united with an understanding equally vigorous and flexible. He was gifted with
70 the faculty of method in the highest degree; and with great powers of application, which were sustained by a prodigious memory: while he could communicate his acquisitions with clear and fluent elocution. . . .

Thus gifted and thus accomplished, Sir Robert Peel had a great
75 deficiency; he was without imagination. Wanting imagination, he wanted prescience. No one was more sagacious when dealing with the circumstances before him; no one penetrated the present with more acuteness and accuracy. His judgment was faultless provided he had not to deal with the future. . . . And so it came to pass that
80 roman catholic emancipation, parliamentary reform, and the abrogation of our commercial system, were all carried out in haste or in passion and without conditions or mitigatory arrangements.

Sir Robert Peel had a peculiarity which is perhaps natural with men of very great talent who have not the creative faculty; he had a
85 dangerous sympathy with the creations of others. Instead of being cold and wary, as was commonly supposed, he was impulsive and ever inclined to rashness. . . .

There are few things more remarkable in parliamentary history than the manner in which Sir Robert Peel headed an opposition for
90 ten years without attempting to form the opinions of his friends, or instilling into them a single guiding principle. . . . He could give to his friends no guiding principle, for he had none, and he kept sitting on those benches till somebody should give him one. . . .

The roman catholic association, the Birmingham Union, the
95 Manchester League, were all the legitimate offspring of Sir Robert Peel. No Minister ever diminished the power of the government in this country so much as this eminent man. No one ever strained the

Constitution so much. He was the unconscious parent of political agitation. He literally forced the people out of doors to become
100 statesmen, and the whole tendency of his policy was to render our institutions mere forms. In a word, no one with all his conservative language more advanced revolution. . . .

One cannot say of Sir Robert Peel, notwithstanding his unrivalled powers of despatching affairs, that he was the greatest
105 minister that this country ever produced, because, twice placed at the helm, and on the second occasion with the Court and the parliament equally devoted to him, he never could maintain himself in power. . . . But what he really was, and what posterity will acknowledge him to have been, is the greatest member of
110 parliament that ever lived.

Peace to his ashes! His name will be often appealed to in that scene which he loved so well, and never without homage even by his opponents.

Benjamin Disraeli, *Lord George Bentinck*, 1905 (first published 1852), pp 198–202, 208

Questions

a What differences of tone are there between Disraeli's criticisms of Peel in extracts *a* and *b*? How do you account for these differences?

★ *b* Identify 'the Birmingham Union (and) the Manchester League' (extract *b*, lines 94, 95). Is it fair of Disraeli to say that Peel let these pressure groups shape government policy?

c What foundations does Disraeli claim for the Conservative Party?

d What strategies are advocated by Disraeli, either explicitly or implicitly, to deal with the challenge of change? See particularly extract *a*, lines 5–9 and extract *b*, lines 81–2.

★ *e* Does the Tamworth Manifesto (section 1, extract *b*) give the lie to Disraeli's assertion in extract *b*, lines 89–91?

f Did Disraeli later, as party leader, carry out the strategies he advocated in 1846 and 1852?

4 Who? Who?

The new Administration were no sooner installed in office than a contest commenced between the opposing parties in Parliament, which was carried on for some time, with skilful tactics on both sides. The object of the Opposition was to extract from the
5 Government a distinct declaration, whether they had or had not abandoned the policy of Protection, anticipating, that whatever answer might be given to this question, the effect would be to damage the Ministry with one or another portion of the public. If,

on the other hand, an abandonment of the cause of commercial
10 restriction were proclaimed, it was reasonably expected that the staunch adherents of that policy in the country, and a large section of the agricultural interest, might take offence at such a desertion of their cause. If, on the other hand, a reversal of the free-trade system were held out, such was the popularity of those principles
15 throughout the country, that it was confidently hoped that an appeal to the people against the reactionary policy of the Government would create a great diversion in favour of their opponents. . . . The Premier stood firm to his originally declared intention of abiding by whatever verdict the country might
20 pronounce at the forthcoming general election on the merits of free trade. . . .

The Chancellor of the Exchequer (Mr. Benjamin Disraeli) replied to the inquiry of Mr. Villiers. Though he questioned the reality of the alarm and distrust to which Mr. Villiers had referred,
25 he was ready to respond frankly to his challenge. Darting a rapid retrospective glance upon the course he had taken with respect to the question of Protection – which, he said, he had distinctly declared, as an abstract question, was no longer to be considered in that House until an appeal had been made to the country – he
30 observed that Her Majesty's present Ministers believed that very great injustice had been done to the agricultural and other interests since 1846, and that it was desirable, for the benefit of all classes, that this injustice should be redressed. But they were not pledged to any specific measures, and, though he would not, to gain
35 popularity, propose in a future Parliament a moderate fixed duty upon corn, yet he would not, to avoid bluster, give it of his opinion that such a duty was one which no Minister, under any circumstances ought to propose; but the proposition should not be made until the verdict of the country had been obtained.

Annual Register, 1852, pp 38–42

Questions

a Identify 'The Premier' referred to in this extract (line 18).

b Comment on the Government's tactics with respect to protection.

★ *c* What was the outcome of the appeal to the country referred to in lines 29 and 39?

d What reasons do this extract and your wider reading suggest for the brevity of Conservative administrations in the 1850s?

5 Lord Derby and Reform

(a) His own analysis

5 March 1867. . . . The state of the reform question and of the

ministry is now more critical than it has been at any former time. There is not, so far as I can judge, much excitement or violence of feeling among the people, but a great deal of interest, and on the
5 part of the educated classes, some not inconsiderable apprehension of possible results. The radical newspapers are of course screaming their loudest. 'The Times' disapproved the resolutions (very naturally) and condemned the bill brought forward a week ago; but is anxious for a bill of some sort to pass, and not averse to its being
10 done by the present government, if that be possible. The party is much divided, but not disinclined to action. My idea is that after two failures we ought to stake everything on this last trick and refuse to accept modifications of the plan, except on points of detail. At the same time we are bound in consistency not to go as
15 far as to effect a real transfer of power to the working class: which would be equally opposed to our interests and ideas. And we must give no plausible colour to the charge (sure to be brought against us) of being ready to support in office what we opposed before. If these conditions are complied with it is not likely that our bill can
20 pass; but we shall have done our duty, and cleared ourselves of further responsibility.

Disraeli, Derby and the Conservative Party. Journals and Memoirs of Edward Henry, Lord Stanley 1849–1869, ed. John Vincent, 1978, p 293

(b) As seen by Lord Kimberley

Oct. 24 [1869] The newspapers announce the death of Lord Derby yesterday morning. I cannot say I think he is a loss as a statesman. His brilliant powers as a debater no one who ever heard him could
25 dispute, but he was impulsive, bitter and unscrupulous, and seldom manifested either sound judgment or accurate knowledge.

It is the fashion to praise his generosity and noble openness of disposition. In debate he certainly seldom showed these qualities during the twenty years I have sat opposite him in the House of
30 Lords. On the contrary no speaker so habitually and glaringly misrepresented his opponents' words. In his political acts he seemed to me to be almost always activated by the reckless spirit of the gambler. Never mind that it is a 'leap in the dark', if we can only 'dish the Whigs'. His whole career was a mass of inconsisten-
35 cies. How the men who could talk as he used to do of having undertaken to stem the tide of democracy, could have made himself responsible as First Minister for the Household suffrage bill, it will puzzle future historians to explain on any hypothesis which does not impugn either his honesty or his courage, or his intelligence.

Camden 3rd Series Vol. 90 (Camden Miscellany Vol. 21), *A*
40 *Journal of Events during the Gladstone Ministry 1864–1874 (1st Earl of Kimberley's Journal*), 1958, p 8

Questions

★ *a* Outline the main events of the passage of the reform bills of 1866 and 1867. Identify the 'two failures' and the 'last trick', referred to in extract *a*, line 12.

b What previous sequence of events might Derby be thinking of when he remarks, 'there is not . . . much excitement or violence of feeling among the people' (extract *a*, lines 3–4)?

★ *c* How deep were the divisions within the Conservative Party to which Derby refers (extract *a*, line 10)? How did they manifest themselves?

d Are there any points of agreement between Derby's assessment of his own position in 1867 (extract *a*), and Kimberley's verdict on Derby (extract *b*)?

★ *e* To what extent was power transferred to the working class by the 1867 Reform Act?

6 Organisation and revival in the 1870s

(a) *The National Union*

THE PRINCIPLES AND OBJECTS OF THE NATIONAL UNION OF CONSERVATIVE AND CONSTITUTIONAL ASSOCIATIONS

THE NATIONAL UNION was established for the purpose of
5 effecting a systematic organisation of Conservative feeling and influence throughout the country, by helping in the formation and work of the Constitutional Associations which have so rapidly increased in numbers. It is notorious that the Constitutional Cause has suffered much from the want of organisation amongst its
10 supporters. Through this want the great conservative strength, which has existed in all parts of the country and in every class of the people, has been deprived of its just influence upon public affairs. It is now obvious that the measure of Reform achieved for the nation by the late Lord Derby and Mr. Disraeli, widening the basis and
15 deepening the foundations of the Constitution, has greatly strengthened the hold of Constitutional principles upon the important constituencies. In all directions – and especially among working men – old Associations have been enlarged and new ones sprung into vigorous life. All that was needed to make them a source of
20 great and abiding strength to the Constitutional cause is that there should be some national organisation ready at all times to give information and advice; to strengthen each Association by combining the influence of all; and to supply a means of bringing to bear upon any public question the united weight of the Constitutional
25 party.

That organisation is found in the NATIONAL UNION.

It was founded in the Autumn of 1867. . . .

The Council, with its various special Committees, has since been meeting constantly, and its work is of a threefold nature.

30 In the first place, it keeps a register of all existing Conservative and Constitutional Associations, with the number of their members, their rules of action, the names and addresses of their officers, and all other particulars which may enable the National Union to act promptly and effectively as their London agency. In the second 35 place, it is always ready to assist with advice, or the personal co-operation of its members, in the service of the existing Associations, or the formation of new ones. . . . Its third class of work is the publication from time to time of short pamphlets on important political questions, and the re-printing of speeches and lectures 40 which may be of enduring and universal interest. . . . During debate on Mr. Gladstone's Irish Church Resolution in 1868 upwards of 37,000 letters and circulars were issued from the office, and 864 petitions, bearing 61,782 signatures, were presented through the Union, a considerably larger number being forwarded 45 direct to Members of Parliament. . . .

Archives of the British Conservative Party, Series One, Pamphlets and Leaflets, Harvester Press, 1977, Microfiche edition, Card 13, 1876/4

(b) Disraeli proclaims a popular agenda

Conservative and Liberal Principles
Speech at Crystal Palace, June 24, 1872

. . . Gentlemen, the Tory party, unless it is a national party is nothing. It is not a confederacy of nobles, it is not a democratic 50 multitude; it is a party formed from all the numerous classes in the realm – classes alike and equal before the law, but whose different conditions and different aims give vigour and variety to our national life. . . .

[Disraeli criticises at length the record of Liberalism and accuses 55 the Liberals of attacks on national institutions.] Now, I have always been of opinion that the Tory party has three great objects. The first is to maintain the institutions of the country – not from any sentiment of political superstition, but because we believe that they embody the principles upon which a community like England can 60 alone safely rest. The principles of liberty, or order of law, and of religion are not to be entrusted to individual opinion or to the caprice and passion of multitudes, but should be embodied in a form of permanence and power. We associate with the Monarchy the ideas which it represents – the majesty of law, the administra-65 tion of justice, the fountains of mercy and of honour. . . .

Gentlemen, there is another and second great object of the Tory party. If the first is to maintain the institutions of the country, the second is, in my opinion to uphold the Empire of England. . . .

Another great object of the Tory party, and one not inferior to 70 the maintenance of the Empire, or the upholding of our institutions, is the elevation of the condition of the people. . . . It must be obvious to all who consider the condition of the multitude with a desire to improve and elevate it, that no important step can be gained unless you can effect some reduction of their hours of labour 75 and humanise their toil. . . . I ventured to say a short time ago, speaking in one of the great cities of this country, that the health of the people was the most important question for a statesman. It is, gentlemen, a large subject. It has many branches. It involves the state of the dwellings of the people. . . . It involves their 80 enjoyment of some of the chief elements of nature – air, light, and water. It involves the regulation of their industry, the inspection of their toil. . . .

Upon you depends the issue. Whatever may be the general feeling, you must remember that in fighting against Liberalism or 85 the Continental system, you are fighting against those who have the advantage of power – against those who have been in high places for nearly half a century. You have nothing to trust to but your own energy and the sublime instinct of an ancient people. You must act as if everything depended on your individual efforts. 90 The secret of success is constancy of purpose. Go to your homes, and teach there these truths, which will soon be imprinted on the conscience of the land. Make each man feel how much rests on his own exertions. . . .

Selected Speeches of the Earl of Beaconsfield, ed. T.E. Kebbel, 1882, pp 23–5, 529, 532, 534–5

(c) Gorst sees his work undone

J.E. Gorst to Disraeli, 2 Dec, 1874

95 You will remember that our victory in the English Boroughs, at the late General Election, was fore-shadowed by successes at the Municipal Elections of 1872 and 1873. I ought therefore to call your attention to the fact that this year we seem, notwithstanding our prestige as the party in office, to be losing the ground which we then 100 gained. . . . We have seen some indication of [a Liberal recovery] in Parliamentary Elections at Stroud, Bath, Hull & elsewhere; and the Municipal Elections of this year appear to furnish additional evidence of the precarious tenure of our position in the Boroughs. . . .

I do not dissent from your view that the mass of the people is, or 105 may be made, Tory. But masses cannot move without leaders; and in English Boroughs we are grievously deficient in Tory leaders. . . .

I was in hopes that the power and patronage which the possession of office has given us might have been to some extent at

least so used as to create in the Boroughs a permanent Tory faction.
110 The Radicals during their long tenure of power sedulously pursued such a policy, and have (I think as a consequence) a staff of Borough leaders immeasurably stronger than ours. But I think your colleagues (who are none of them Borough Members themselves) either fail to see the necessity for such a policy or
115 despair of maintaining permanently our position in the Boroughs. At any rate little has been done to strengthen & consolidate our friends in the Boroughs and much to alienate and discourage them. . . .

Disraeli Papers B/XX1/D/463a, quoted in H.J. Hanham, *Elections and Party Management: Politics in the time of Disraeli and Gladstone*, 1959, pp 389–90

(d) 'Two Nations' in one party

TORY DEMOCRACY [A response by J.E. Gorst to Lord
120 Rosebery's book on Lord Randolph Churchill]
. . . . In 1868 the Tory party received a crushing defeat at the general election. Many thought it would be in Opposition for at least a generation, and the aristocratic section abandoned the field in despair. But Mr. Disraeli with a few colleagues set diligently to
125 work to reorganize the broken party. This was done upon strictly democratic lines. The principles of Tory Democracy were proclaimed in speech and pamphlet, and working men's Conservative associations were established all over the country to propagate them; an organization representing all classes was established in
130 each constituency to choose Parliamentary Candidates and conduct elections; it was an embryo caucus from which the complete system was afterwards developed by Mr. Schnadhorst. . . . [Disraeli, says Gorst, was mistrusted by many wealthier tories as a radical and socialist.] But so did not think the democratic section
135 which he had organized. The Conservative working men gave him the majority of 1874, the only Tory majority there has been since the days of Peel. The whole party then, as Lord Rosebery says, 'fell down and worshipped'. The aristocratic section, which had despaired of Toryism in 1868, returned; most of the 'spoils' fell to
140 them, and they showed no reluctance to reap that which others had sown [Gorst goes on to claim Lord Randolph Churchill as the defender of 'Tory Democracy' against the later tendency of the Conservatives to exploit popular support in the interests of the upper classes].
145 Yours truly, JOHN E. GORST

At sea, off Australia, Dec. 30 [1906]

The Times, 6 Feb 1907

Questions

a Why was the Conservative Party alternatively called the Constitutional Party (extract *a*)?

b What were the main strengths and weaknesses of Conservative Party organisation in the 1870s as revealed by these extracts?

★ *c* To what extent was the Crystal Palace agenda translated into a programme for Government after 1874?

d How consistent are Gorst's assessments of the forces at work within the Conservative Party as he saw them in 1874 and in retrospect (extracts *c* and *d*)?

e In what ways does Gorst allow subsequent events and trends to colour his analysis in retrospect (extract *d*)? In particular, is it reasonable to describe the Conservative Party machinery in 1874 as an embryo caucus (line 131)? (See also Chapter 4, section 6.)

IV *The Liberal Party from Peel to Gladstone*

The genesis of the Liberal Party is even harder to identify than that of the Conservative Party. Lord Blake attributes it to the coming together of Whigs, Peelites and Radicals in opposition to Derby's 1859 ministry. This coalescence has been traced in detail in John Vincent's study of the period 1857–68. Other studies have laid particular emphases: J.B. Conacher's study of the Peelites shows that eventually, many of the Peelites left the scene or were reabsorbed into the Tory party. T.A. Jenkins' recent study of Gladstone, Whiggery and the Liberal Party, gives a higher profile and greater durability to the 'whigs' up to 1886.

Every major political party is to some extent an uneasy coalition of interests. In the Liberal party were placed the hopes and aspirations of many reformers, while there lingered also an aristocratic concept of government which was finally lost to the Unionists in the person of Lord Hartington, successor to Lords Grey, Melbourne, Russell and Palmerston.

In the quarter century before 1874, the Liberal Party gained and retained the support of a preponderance of the Press, of nonconformity and of the trade unions. During the uncharacteristic interlude of Lord Palmerston's ascendency it was even associated with a forward foreign policy. Yet, by a certain irony, when Gladstone set about reform in Ireland and at home in earnest, the party began to alienate its natural supporters to some degree.

How was the party rescued for a further electoral victory in 1880? Was it due more to Gladstone's impassioned electioneering or to new methods of organisation in the boroughs, especially Birmingham under Chamberlain?

John Vincent proposes, not altogether sympathetically, that a Liberal majority throughout the late nineteenth century would have been 'natural'. Every departure from that condition is therefore attributable to some alienating policy at home, in Ireland or abroad, internal dissension or the new allure of socialism. Lord Rosebery stated both the strength and the epitaph of the Liberal Party when he said in Stratford in 1894,

> I believe the Liberal Party is never destroyed or defeated except by itself, and that it is only defections, or schism, or apathy or disunion inside the Liberal Party that can cause it any serious apprehensions of defeat.

1 Gladstone in Peel's Government

Aug. 31 [18]41. In consequence of a note received this morning from Sir Robert Peel I went to him at half past eleven. The following is the substance of a quarter of an hour's conversation. He said,

5 'In this great struggle in which we have been and are to be engaged, the chief importance will attach to questions of finance. It would not be in my power to undertake the business of Chancellor of the Exchequer in detail. I therefore have asked [Henry] Goulburn to fill that office and I shall be simply First Lord. I think 10 we shall be very strong in the House of Commons if as a part of this arrangement you will accept the post of Vice President of the Board of Trade and conduct the business of that great department in the House of Commons with Lord Ripon as President. I consider it an office of the highest importance, and you will have my 'unbounded 15 confidence' in it.

I said, 'of the importance and responsibility of that office at the present time I am well aware: but it is right that I should say as simply as I can, that I really am not fit for it. I have no special knowledge of trade whatever; with a few questions I am 20 acquainted, but they are such as have come across me incidentally; speaking not all in vague professions of incompetency nor as modesty might dictate, but as matter of fact, it is the case that my mind has not been accustomed or turned to them, they have not been among my pursuits'.

25 He said, 'The satisfactory conduct of an office of that kind must after all depend more upon the intrinsic qualities of the man, than upon the precise amount of his personal knowledge. . . .'

He resumed, 'if there be any other arrangement that you would prefer, my value and affectionate regard for you would make me 30 most desirous to effect it so far as the claims of others would permit – to be perfectly frank and unreserved, I should tell you, that there are many reasons which would have made me wish to send you to Ireland but upon the whole I think that had better not be done – some considerations 'connected with the Presbyterians of Ireland' 35 make me prefer on the whole that we should adopt a different plan. . . .

[Gladstone continues to plead incompetence, especially in matters of military and naval economics, but accepts Peel's offer with a final reservation about policy towards China and opium.]

40 It has always been my hope, that I might be able to avoid this class of public employments: on this account I have not endeavoured to train myself for them: the place is very distasteful to me, and which is of more importance I fear I may hereafter demonstrate the unfitness I have today only stated. However it comes to me, I think, as a matter of plain duty: it may be all the

better for not being according to my own best planning: and I must forthwith go to work, in sum, as a reluctant schoolboy meaning well – .

British Library, Add. MS 44819, folios 69–71

Questions

★ *a* In the light of events before and after Peel's 1841 election victory, comment on the phrase, 'the chief importance will attach to questions of finance' (line 6).

b Compare Gladstone's professed attitude to this offer of a post with his privately expressed feelings. Are there any shades of difference between what he says and what he thinks?

★ *c* What difficulties might Gladstone have had in religious relationships if he had become Irish Secretary? You might cite his stance over the Maynooth grant as a case.

d What advantages would Gladstone derive from keeping detailed political memoranda? What is the value of these items of evidence to historians?

★ *e* What political priorities might Peel and Gladstone have shared, but which set them at odds with the 'high tories' in the party?

2 The Peelites

(a) In Peel's lifetime

[Sir James] Graham to [Sir Robert] Peel: January 15th [1848].

I have no faith whatever in the possibility of reuniting under any cricumstances the party which you led in 1841.

Implicit reliance on your superior judgment, honesty, and
5 prudence was the keystone of that great combination. The different shades of opinion in that party were very numerous, but the whole was blended in the confidence which you inspired, and in the general conviction that you were the man most fit to govern. That confidence is now abjured, and without it the party is dissolved
10 into its first elements, which are most discordant.

Time will probably solve the difficulty, and will restore order to chaos, by fresh combinations, not by the revival of past agreements, never to be renewed.

C.S. Parker, *Life and Letters of Sir James Graham*, pub. John Murray, London, 1907, Vol. II, pp 63–4

(b) After Peel's death

9 Sept. 1897

When the sad and unexpected death of Sir R. Peel occurred in 1850,
15 it became necessary to consider whether his followers still

constituted a party. They were not in general prepared for absorption in either of the two great parties, the Government and the Protectionists. One among us, namely Lord Lincoln, was so sanguine as to believe that we were destined to be a lasting and
20 gowing party: that we were to attract the best men from all sides, and after a time to govern the country. These I [*sic*: read 'high'] expectations I never shared nor in any manner encouraged. Lord Aberdeen as a peer was less concerned with ideas of this kind; and Sir James Graham stood rather aloof from us, and was more readily
25 prepared for what would have been for him simply a renewal of his old and original party alliance with the Whigs or Liberals. . . .

It had . . . become essential for the Peelites, if we were to have even for the shortest time a separate existence, to be under a leader. I found that the Duke of Newcastle coveted this post. It appeared to
30 me that Lord Aberdeen was on every ground the person entitled to hold it. I made my views distinctly known to the Duke. He took no offence. I do not know what communications he may have held with others. But the upshot was Lord Aberdeen became our leader. And this result was obtained without any shock or conflict. . . .

British Library, Add. MS 44791, folios 70–102, quoted in *The Prime Ministers' Papers Series: W.E. Gladstone, I. Autobiographica:* ed. John Brooke and Mary Sorensen, 1971, pp 71–2

Questions

a What were the 'first elements' into which the Conservative party had dissolved (extract *a*, line 9)?

b In what ways do Graham's contemporary opinions and Gladstone's later recollections differ in their assessments of the Peelites' prospects?

c In what ways did Peel's death alter the Peelites' circumstances?

* *d* Did 'time . . . solve the difficulty . . . by fresh combinations' (extract *a*, line 11)?

e What light do these extracts shed on the place of party in politics in the late 1840s and early 1850s?

3 Palmerston

Mr. [Charles] Greville to [Sir James] Graham
December 29th 1851

You know all that passed about the reception of Kossuth, and the Islington deputation and speeches. Upon this latter affair a correspondence took place between [Lord] John [Russell] and Pam; the former remonstrated, the latter defended himself. The queen
5 resented it, but in the end it was patched up by their affecting to believe Palmerston's denials, and his promising to behave better for

the future. They were afraid to face Kossuth and anti-Austrian excitement, and to cast him on Radical support, against what would have been called 'foreign interference' and 'slavish submis-
10 sion to Russia and Austria'. So the storm passed over, and he remained as usual 'immortal and unchanged'.

Then came the French coup d'état, when without consulting anybody he expressed to Walewski [French Ambassador in London] his unqualified approbation of the President's [Louis
15 Napoleon's] acts. This Walewski instantly wrote to Turgot [French Foreign Minister].

Meanwhile Normanby [British Ambassador in Paris], who had given offence to the President by language of an unfriendly character, wrote home for instructions. At a Cabinet, it was
20 determined that he should be instructed to express no opinion, and to take a reserved but not unfriendly attitude – one, in short, of perfect neutrality, taking no part and waiting to see the result – and Palmerston was to write to him in that sense.

This resolution was taken down to the Queen at Osborne, after
25 which the Ministers separated. Soon after Normanby wrote to John Russell in great indignation, complaining of the usage he had received from Palmerston, who had written him a strong letter rebuking him for his language, and hinting that the President would most likely ask for his recall. At the same time Normanby
30 informed Lord John that Turgot had shown him Walewski's despatch conveying Palmerston's entire approbation.

In addition to this the remonstrance of the three Cabinets [Austria, Prussia and Russia] about the refugees [Kossuth etc.] was presented to Palmerston, who put it in his pocket, and never said a
35 word to anybody about it.

On receiving these accounts from Normanby Lord John Russell thought it time to finish with Palmerston, went off to the Queen and settled it. He then wrote a letter, asking for explanations, informing him that the Queen was greatly displeased, and desired
40 to place the foreign office in other hands. . . . [Palmerston was dismissed and succeeded by Lord Granville].

C.S. Parker, *Life and Letters of Sir James Graham*, pub. John Murray, 1907, Vol. II, pp 145–6

Questions

★ *a* Explain the references in paragraph one to Kossuth, and the Islington deputation.

★ *b* Explain the references in paragraph two to the French *coup d'état*.

c Trace in this letter some of the roots of Palmerston's unpopularity with the court and some colleagues.

d Can you detect also clues to his popularity in the country?

★ *e* To what extent did the policies and actions of Lord John Russell and Lord Palmerston delay the integration of Gladstone and the Peelites with the Liberal Party in the 1850s and 1860s?

4 1868: The Liberal Party comes of age

. . . The results [of the 1868 election] in some respect falsified the expectations of all parties. In the English boroughs with certain exceptions, the Liberal party achieved a decided success, and largely increased their majority. In the English counties, alike in 5 those in which manufacturing and those where agricultural interests predominated, the Conservatives obtained many signal triumphs. In Scotland, again, the candidates of the latter party suffered extraordinary reverses. . . . Of the whole number of representatives returned by Scotland seven only were Conserva-10 tives. In Ireland also the Liberal party gained a decided, though not so overwhelming an advantage. Some of the boroughs in the province of Ulster in which the Presbyterian influence prevails were for the first time won by the Liberals.

The aggregate result of the elections produced an important 15 accession to the strength of that party which acknowledged Mr. Gladstone as leader, and adhered to his project of disestablishing the Irish Church. According to the best computation it would appear that the Liberals gained in the whole fifteen seats, which is equivalent to thirty votes on a division. The relative strength of the 20 two parties in the new Parliament was estimated as follows: – Liberals 387, Conservatives 272. But though the net result was thus favourable to the former party, their triumph was somewhat marred by considerable local defeats, and by the rejection of some of the most eminent members of the Liberal ranks, especially by 25 that of Mr. Gladstone himself. Despising the easy success which he might have obtained with a smaller constituency that gentleman had fearlessly appealed to the great electoral division of South-West Lancashire, and had in several powerful speeches addressed to large multitudes of the constituents endeavoured to gain their support to 30 the cause on which he had staked the issue. On the other hand great and weighty influences both of property and of opinion were efficiently worked against him, the efforts of the clergy being especially active in the defence of what they considered the sacred cause of the Irish Church. The election, which was attended with 35 much excitement and was watched with extraordinary interest throughout the Kingdom, terminated as follows:–

For Mr. Cross, Conservative 7729
Mr. Turner, Conservative 7676
Mr. Gladstone, Liberal 7415
Mr. Grenfell, Liberal 6939

. . . It was fortunate for Mr. Gladstone that the contingency of his defeat, not wholly unanticipated, had been provided for by the zeal of his friends in another numerous constituency. His return for 40 the borough of Greenwich in conjunction with another Liberal member, Alderman Salomons, had been previously secured. . . .

Annual Register, 1868, pp 171–2

Questions

a Comment on the opening sentence of this extract.
b What light does the extract shed on the class and regional bases of support for the two parties?
c Which Irish group other than Catholics supported Irish Church disestablishment?
d Does the extract and treatment of Gladstone's candidancy in Lancashire reveal the writer's political bias?
★ *e* How would the national public have followed the 1868 election campaign?
f What evidence is there that, in two-member constituencies, party loyalties were not absolute?
★ *g* Does this extract help us to ascertain the limitations of electoral calculations and predictions in this period?

5 Leadership

[Three letters by Gladstone to Lord Granville]

11 Carlton House Terrace Jan 13/[18]75

The time had, I think arrived when I ought to revert to the subject of the letter which I addressed to you on the 12th of March [1874: proposing resignation from leadership].

Before determining whether I should offer to assume a change, 5 which might extend over a length of time, I have reviewed, with all the care in my power, a number of considerations both public and private, of which a portion, and these not by any means insignificant, were not in existence at the date of that letter.

The result has been that I see no public advantage in my 10 continuing to act as the leader of the Liberal Party; and that at the age of sixty-five, and after forty-two years of a laborious public life, I think myself entitled to retire on the present opportunity. This retirement is dictated to me by my personal views as to the best method of spending the closing years of my life. . . .

Hawarden Castle Jan 17/[18]75

15 [About a meeting to choose a successor:] it should be like a meeting which was held automatically after the defeat in 1866 – unless, and until, some arrangement is made which it may be thought wise to propose or support from your quarter, but I would not give this

sort of character to the meeting as such and in the first instance.
20 In general, leadership has been I think spontaneously rather than formally determined. And in your good management I dare say Hartington will get quietly into the saddle, or rather upon the pillion. . . .

Hawarden Castle Jan 27/[18]75

I am sorry, rather than surprised, to hear of difficulties about the
25 choice [between Hartington and Forster] of a leader in the Commons; not because there is any difficulty in the act, but because of the condition and habits of those who have to perform it. I received this morning from Kinnaird a note, in which he says that there is to be a fight for it and that it will not be very creditable.
30 It will indeed be the very last degree of the ridiculous to which a party can be reduced, and for party purposes matter of ridicule weighs more than dishonour. I do hope measures will be taken to prevent men from making fools of themselves at the meeting next week. The dictate of common sense seems to me plain enough. If
35 the party are not generally agreed some friends of the respective candidates, or non-candidates, should agree to adjourn the meeting, without any thing approaching to debate, for further, consideration of the subject. There are two dangers: one a public squabble, the other an unreal conclusion and appointment. There is
40 but one good thing that such a meeting can do: namely to register with marked signs of unanimity and loyalty a foregone conclusion. To imagine it to be deliberative, while it is headless, is I think a fatal error. Supposing they are not prepared to agree, the party can do for a time without a leader in the Commons. The truth is, it has
45 peccant humours to purge, and bad habits to get rid of, and it is a great question whether this can or cannot be best done without first choosing a leader. . . .

The Political Correspondence of Mr. Gladstone and Lord Granville 1868–1876, ed. Agatha Ramm, Camden 3rd Series Vol. 82, pp 464–8

Questions

a What was 'the present opportunity' (line 12)?

★ *b* What activities did Gladstone plan to turn to in 'the closing years of . . . life' (line 14)?

c What weaknesses in party structure are revealed in these letters?

d Why might Gladstone have disliked competitive elections for leadership?

★ *e* How far had Gladstone's own personal style of leadership, and the personalities of those he led, contributed to the problem of choosing a leader in the Commons in 1875?

6 The Birmingham caucus

After the passing of the Reform Bill [1867] the leaders of the Liberal party in Birmingham recognised the new conditions under which alone success would be possible. They saw the absolute necessity of taking their party *as a whole* into their direct and intimate confidence. It was evident to them that the day had gone by for attempting to control a large constituency by cliques composed of a few wealthy men. A whole suburb could be outvoted by a couple of streets. Previous efforts had been directed towards the formation on a wide basis of a superior kind of election committee upon which representatives of various sections of the community should act, and which should secure its own harmony by carefully avoiding troublesome questions and confining its work to the support of certain candidates for seats in parliament.

It was soon perceived that the development of the life of a great town needs some agency far more powerful and more worthy than a mere election committee, waking up at certain intervals, and managed by the repetition of party cries. Electioneering in many constituencies, apart from bribery and corruption, had consisted chiefly in the loud utterance of watchwords to a crowd secretly regarded as 'vulgar', and in the ingenious invention of inducements sufficiently strong to drive the despised mob to the polling booth.

Time, trouble and thought were not simply spent, but lavished in Birmingham – by not a few men beyond the limits of health and strength – to persuade the people at large that political interests are the interests of civilisation in its broadest sense. The improvement of the dwellings of the poor; the promotion of temperance; the multiplication of libraries and art galleries; the management of grammar schools, as well as public elementary schools, were all discussed as questions of Liberal politics, that is, as questions which challenged the organised action of the community through its various representative assemblies. . . .

Educational institutions, it was also insisted, must be under 'Liberal' direction – by a 'Liberal' direction being understood resistance to denominational agency and the widest possible extension of the school board system under which the ratepayers control the education of their own children.

It was further contended that the interests of all representative institutions are so intermingled, and the lines of their practical work so often cross and recross each other, that a 'Liberal' representation in the House of Commons could not be placed beyond doubt, without the election of a 'Liberal' school board and a 'Liberal' town council. . . .

Rev. W. Crosskey on the '600' of Birmingham, *Macmillan's Magazine*, Vol. XXXV, Nov. 1876–Apr. 1877, pp 1301–2, quoted in *English Historical Documents*, Vol. XII(2), 1874–1914, ed. W.D. Handcock, 1977, pp 70–72.

Questions

- *a* With which major Liberal party figure were these organisational changes associated?
- *b* These changes in party organisation are represented as democratisation. As 'caucus' politics, in what ways were these changes viewed by antagonists?
- ★ *c* Identify an example in this extract of the exploitation by Liberals at a local level of legislation passed by a Conservative government.
- ★ *d* Why and how did this degree of party organisation in Birmingham turn to the Liberal's disadvantage after 1886?

7 The 1880s: Radical and Socialist programmes

(a) A Radical programme

What Remains to be Done.

Reform of the Land Laws: to enable land to be bought and sold cheaply; to convert ninety-nine years building leases into freeholds; to enable any man to buy and cultivate small lots of land as peasant
5 farmer.

Technical Education: to establish schools for teaching handicrafts to workmen.

Reform of the Licensing Laws: to enable the ratepayers of each town or district to regulate its own drink traffic.

10 Women's suffrage: to place women on an equality with men in the exercise of the right of voting for Members of Parliament.

Improved Dwellings for the Poor in towns, with cheap early trains for workmen.

Reform of Parliamentary Procedure: members to be paid, sitting
15 during the day instead of after dark; abolition of verbal questioning of Ministers, &c.

The Reform or Abolition of the House of Lords.

Disestablishment of the Church of England. . . .

Triennial Parliaments. . . .

20 Financial Reform: to abolish all perpetual pensions, such as £4000 a year for ever to the heirs of the Duke of Marlborough, who died 170 years ago. . . .

Army and Navy Reforms: to give us a better and cheaper army in return for the £20,000,000 we spend every year over our army,
25 and to reduce the number of Generals (591) and Admirals (309). To increase the efficiency of the volunteers, upon whom (200,000 men) the Government spends £375,600 a year, whilst 442 Generals alone absorb £368,457.

Parliamentary Reform: to secure a better representation of the
30 people, and less preponderance of the landed interest, the fighting

interest, official interests, railway interest, &c. . . .

Income Tax. . . . Every man should pay according to his means, and the rich man at a higher rate than the poor man.

Taxes on tea, coffee and cocoa, which now yield 4½ millions and
35 are all paid by the poor, should be abolished.

Poor Rates. . . . Every man should contribute to poor rates according to his income . . . and not according to the rent he pays. . . .

Nationalization of the Land. . . . (*This is not mentioned here as
40 forming part of the programme of the Liberal party. Many people think it impracticable).

Frederick A. Binney, *What Liberals have done for the Country: A few words to Conservative Working Men*, 1884, pp 19–20, Pamphlets at St Deiniol's Library, Hawarden, 78/J/6

(b) A Socialist programme

What can be done to dispel the political apathy of London? How can a renewal of the crushing Liberal defeats of 1885 and 1886 be averted? These are questions which must constantly be rising in the
45 minds of earnest workers for Liberalism in the great metropolitan centre. . . .

One proof of this political indifference of the mass of the people is furnished by the Registration and Polling Statistics. 'London is not on the Register', says Mr. Seager, and this in spite of an
50 enormously increased diligence and activity of most of the parish officials. The 60 London Constituencies (including West Ham, but excluding the University) had in 1881, a population of 3,946,139; in 1885 probably 4,250,000. Among them there would be over a million adult males. Less than half of these (497,841) were on the
55 1885 register. . . .

Still more significant is the geographical distribution of the electoral apathy. Taking still the 1885 figures, the smallest percentage of registered electors who polled is found in Haggerston, and next in 'this bad eminence' rank Hoxton, Stepney,
60 Holborn, East Finsbury, St. George's in the East, South West Ham, South West Bethnal Green, Mile End, Poplar, Central Finsbury, Bow and North East Bethnal Green. The indifference of industrial London to Liberalism could not be more graphically pictured. . . .

65 [Webb challenges the Liberal Party with a programme:]

We profess to desire to remove the grievances of the workers. We ask for their votes to aid us in setting Ireland free so as to enable us then to work out their redemption. . . .

The Programme for London:

70 . . . Complete shifting of burden [of taxation] from the workers, of whatever grade, to the recipients of rent and interest, with a

view to the ultimate and gradual extinction of the latter class. . . . Abolition of all customs and excise duties, except those on Spirits. . . . Increase of income tax; differentiating in favour of
75 earned as against unearned incomes and graduating cumulatively by system of successive levels of abatement. . . . Equalisation and increase of death duties. . . . Shifting of local rates and house duty from occupier to owner. . . .

Extension of the general provisions of the Factory and Work-
80 shops Acts . . . to all employers of labour. . . .

Educational Reform . . . to enable all, even the poorest, children to obtain not merely some but the best education they are capable of. . . . The immediate abolition of all fees in public elementary schools, Board or voluntary, with a corresponding increase in the
85 Government grant. . . . Creation of a Minister for Education. . . . Provision of public technical and secondary schools wherever needed, and creation of abundant public secondary scholarships. . . .

Reorganisation of Poor Law Administration. . . . The separation
90 of the relief of the aged and the sick from the workhouse system, by a universal system of aged pensions, and public infirmaries. . . . The industrial organisation and technical education of all able-bodied paupers. . . . The provision of temporary relief works for the unemployed. . . . The supersession of the Boards of Guardians
95 by the local municipal authorities.

Extension of Municipal Activity. . . .

Reform of registration so as to give a vote, both Parliamentary and municipal, to every adult. . . . Annual Parliaments. . . . Payment of election expenses. . . . Payment of all public represen-
100 tatives. . . . Second ballot [eliminating low-polling candidates until a candidate secures an absolute majority?]. . . . Abolition or painless extinction of House of Lords.

Every one of the proposals in this programme has been individually approved by Liberal leaders of high political standing.
105 What is in question is how much of it the party is yet prepared for. . . .

Sidney Webb, *Wanted, a Programme: An Appeal to the Liberal Party, The Labour Press*, 1888, p 3–5, 13–16, Pamphlets at St Deiniol's Library, Hawarden, 78/J/7

Questions

a In what respect do these two programmes vary in detail and in principle?

★ *b* Was it fair of Webb to refer to the 1885 and 1886 elections as 'crushing Liberal defeats' (extract *b*, line 43)?

c What evidence does Webb use to assert that working men did not feel adequately represented by the Liberal Party?

d What priority does Webb's programme share with the contemporary Gladstonian Liberal programme?

8 Forward to the 1890s

[Speech at Islington by Sir William Harcourt, 26 June 1891]

. . . The policy of the Liberal Party is a policy which is to last for ever in its work. It is not one of those catchpenny expedients, got up at any moment to suit the political market or to serve the
5 purpose of an election. It initiates principles and proclaims reforms which take a long time to give effect to, and every one of those reforms has powerful and selfish interests to encounter. It is a far-seeing and far-reaching policy. At its outset it alarms the selfishness and offends the sentiments of powerful interests. The Tory party is
10 the Party of Privilege and Monopoly. It lives in constant dread lest its well-fenced park should be invaded by the vulgar herd. Every reform is assailed from its first appearance by every kind of prejudice and outcry, bred of rage and terror. Every argument, every bugbear is paraded which can alarm the timid or incense the
15 greedy and invoke fears and hatred against the invader. You are told that the Constitution is in danger, you are told that the Monarchy will fall, you are told that the lawn sleeves of the Bishops may be imperilled, and the Empire crumble into dust (Laughter). This is what Mr. Goschen called the old game – we
20 know it well. . . . All the old reforms have been carried inspite of the same outcry, the same threats, the same terrors. That is the past history of reform. It is the history of to-day. And it will be the history of reforms yet unborn and hardly yet conceived in the womb of time. . . . Who would have said two years ago that we
25 were going to have Free Education? (Laughter). Who would have anticipated many of these reforms? Do not, therefore, be cast down when you see the hurricane of abuse poured upon any Liberal reforms. Be certain that if the Liberal party do not carry it out the Tory party will (Laughter).

Archives of the British Liberal Party, Harvester Press, 1978, Microfiche edition, card 11, 1891/3, pp 12–14

Questions

a What criticisms of Liberalism is Harcourt aiming to disarm?

* *b* Why is Harcourt's quotation from Goschen tinged with irony?

c Are there instances in this period of the Tories 'stealing the Liberals' clothes' in the way Harcourt suggests?

V Domestic Policies and Reforms 1868–80

This chapter provides an opportunity to relate the political activity of the 1870s to its wider context in social and economic change. The issues raised in debate and tackled by legislation during Gladstone's and Disraeli's ministries of 1868–80 are many: the urbanisation and industrialisation of Britain met responses in trade union, public health and factory legislation. There is also a connection between democratisation, industrialisation and the establishment of elementary education for all. This in turn generates a debate based on the three-cornered conflict between Anglicanism, non-conformity and secularism. Developments in warfare – European, colonial and naval – stimulate military reform, while an almost Napoleonic concept of 'the career open to people of talent' underpins the reforms in the universities, civil service and armed forces.

What philosophy supports the programmes of the Liberals and Conservatives? As one would expect there are keys to Gladstone's reforms: justice for Ireland, efficiency, broadening of opportunity. In Disraeli's case the matter has been more open to debate. Are Disraeli's reforms a flowering of 'tory democracy' – a logical conclusion of the youthful aspirations of the Young Englander – or are they a product of the moment – of political opportunism and electoral calculation? Are they an embodiment of the ideas proposed at the Crystal Palace in 1872, or a rag-bag of measures with no foundation?

The question could be put this way. Was there a consensus in the 1870s about the way forward? Did these two governments vie with each other to make the changes that many people agreed were due, or were their programmes in conflict with each other, so that one ministry undid the work of the other, as has happened at times in the twentieth century? In either case, which contemporary attitudes, social, cultural, religious, philosophical, did each party lay claim to?

Social progress in the 1870s speaks for itself. It was not radical or rapid, but by 1880 much permanent change had been brought about by legislation. As to the ministries and parties, however, it is as important to study their failures as their success. Gladstone's ministry was brought down by the tendency of its programme to alienate some and disappoint others, and the exhaustion of its legislating efforts after 1872 heightened these anxieties rather than allaying them. Disraeli's government ran into economic misfortune such as bad harvests, and, of course, both governments drew fire for their foreign policies, which are studied in Chapter VI. It has often been suggested that Disraeli, in particular, was attempting to buy the support of the mass electorate, but in the end, as Robert Blake remarks, 'gratitude is not a characteristic of voters'.

1 Hail. . .

(a) Gladstone's programme

16 February 1869

The LORD CHANCELLOR delivered HER MAJESTY'S Speech to both Houses of Parliament as follows:–

'My Lords, and Gentlemen,

5 . . . it is with special interest that I commend to you the resumption of your labours at a time when the popular branch of the legislature has been chosen with the advantage of a greatly enlarged enfranchisement of My faithful and loyal people.

I am able to inform you that My relations with all foreign powers 10 continue to be most friendly, and I have the satisfaction to believe that they cordially share in the desire by which I am animated for the maintenance of peace. . . .

[A settlement between Greece and Turkey has been attempted].

I have been engaged in negotiations with the United States of 15 North America for the settlement of questions which affect the interests and the international relations of the two countries. . . .

[Events in New Zealand cause anxiety. Reform is promised in the areas of armed forces spending, conduct of elections, rates, Scottish and Endowed schools and bankruptcy. It is hoped that 20 Habeas Corpus need not again be suspended in Ireland].

The Ecclesiastical arrangements of Ireland will be brought under your consideration at a very early date, and the legislation which will be necessary in order to their final adjustment will make the largest demands upon the wisdom of Parliament. . . .'

Hansard, Third Series, Vol. CXCIV, 1869, Columns 24–6

(b) Disraeli's programme

25 24 June 1875

(Disraeli) It may be all very well for hon. and right hon. Gentlemen to treat with affected contempt the notion that our legislation should be founded on permission, but permissive legislation is the characteristic of a free people. It is easy to adopt compulsory

30 legislation when you have to deal with those who only exist to obey; but in a free country, and especially in a country like England, you must trust to persuasion and example as the two great elements, if you wish to effect any considerable change in the manners and customs of the people.

Hansard, Third Series, Vol. CCXXV, 1875, Column 525

Questions

a Why is there so little mention of major domestic reform in the Queen's speech of 1869 (extract *a*)? Which major reforms of 1869–74 are foreseen?

★ *b* How justified would voters in 1874 have been in feeling that the original programme of Gladstone's ministry had been departed from?

★ *c* In what ways does the assessment of foreign affairs made by the Queen and her ministers seem complacent in retrospect?

d Is Disraeli's defence of 'permissive legislation' adequate? What were the main areas of domestic reform between 1874 and 1880 which fall into this category? Did this model of reform prove to be effective?

2 The Army

(a) Earl Russell's proposals

1. That not less than 200,000 men, consisting of regular army and embodied militia, should be kept up within the United Kingdom.
2. Army – That the system of purchase of commissions in the army should be abolished, either immediately or gradually.
5 3. That to the Commander-in-Chief should be assigned, as at present, the duties of maintaining discipline in the army and of recommending officers for promotion.
4. That the field artillery should be largely increased, according to the example of Prussia.
10 5. That a sufficient store of powder should be provided both for artillery and infantry.
6. That the recruiting of privates for the artillery should be stimulated by bounty.
7. That the term of service, both for infantry and cavalry, should
15 be for seven years, and for artillery for ten years.
8. That a service of twenty-one years should entitle the soldier to a pension of 9d[pence], and of twenty-four years of 1s[a shilling] a day.

[Points 9–12 concern the militia].

Annual Register, 1871, p 21, quoting a letter to *The Times*

(b) Cardwell defends the use of the Royal Warrant

Tantallon House,
North Berwick,
8th August 1871.

My dear Cardwell,

20 . . . I have never expressed myself to anyone in private on the subject of the Army Bill or the Royal Warrant in a manner different from that in which I have spoken to yourself, or so as in any way to account for the introduction of my name into Tuesday's debate. I have always thought and said that the issuing of such a warrant was 25 within the undoubted power of the Crown, though to do so without having a sufficient assurance that Parliament would provide the necessary compensation for the officers who otherwise suffer from such an exercise of royal power would not be just, and, therefore, would not be consistent with the spirit of the constitu- 30 tion, which vests all such powers in the Crown, in the confidence and for the purpose that right, not wrong, shall be done. I should have been glad if it had been generally and clearly understood from the beginning that, subject to the sense of Parliament being ascertained with reference to the point of compensation, the form 35 of procedure would be that which was eventually adopted; because it is certainly an evil that the adoption of one constitutional mode of procedure rather than another should appear to arise from an adverse vote of the House of Lords. . . .

Yours etc.
[Sir] Roundell Palmer [afterwards Earl of Selborne, Liberal Lord Chancellor].

30th August 1871.

My dear Palmer,

. . . My present purpose is to raise an enquiry on that part of [Palmer's letter], which suggests that we might as well have issued 40 the Warrant at first, and only have asked for the money. Have you not overlooked the consideration, which we regarded as cardinal, that we could not ask the House of Commons for money to pay the prohibited prices, in any form than by a Bill, to which the House of Lords should be a party?

45 . . . When they [the Lords] passed the suspensory resolution [effectively 'killing off' the Commons' vote to end purchase of commission], we used the power of the Crown, backed by the pecuniary support of the House of Commons, and threw it back upon the Lords to determine how far that support should be drawn 50 upon. If the Lords had continued obstinate, we could only have asked the House of Commons for the regulation prices, until such

time as reason should dawn again upon the horizon of the House of Lords. Ever yours.

Edward Cardwell

General Sir Robert Biddulph (Cardwell's military secretary), *Lord Cardwell at the War Office*, 1904, pp 258–60.

Questions

a What external events prompted the government's interest in army reform in 1871? Where are these events hinted at in Russell's plan (extract *a*)?

★ *b* How closely did Cardwell's plan follow Russell's? How far beyond Russell's plan did Cardwell's reforms go?

c Does Palmer (extract *b*) object in principle to the use of the Royal Warrant, or in practice in this case?

★ *d* From which directions did the strongest resistance to Cardwell's army reforms and the use of the Royal Warrant come?

3 Unwillingly to school?

(a) The 1870 Act

1. This Act may be cited as 'The Elementary Education Act, 1870.'

----

5. There shall be provided for every school district a sufficient amount of accommodation in public elementary schools (as herein-
5 after defined) available for all the children resident in such district for whose elementary education efficient and suitable provision is not otherwise made, and where there is an insufficient amount of such accommodation . . . the deficiency shall be supplied in manner provided by this Act.

10 6. Where the Education Department, in the manner provided by this Act, were satisfied and have given public notice that there is an insufficient amount of public school accommodation for any school district, and the deficiency is not supplied as herein-after required, a school board shall be formed for such district. . . .

15 7. . . . (1) It shall not be required, as a condition of any child being admitted into or continuing in the school, that he shall abstain from attending any Sunday school, or any place of religious worship, or that he shall attend any religious subjects in the school or
20 elsewhere. . . .

(2) The time or times during which any religious

observance is practised or instruction in religious subjects is given at any meeting of the school shall be either at the beginning or at the end or at the beginning and the end of such meeting . . . and any scholar may be withdrawn by his parent from such observance or instruction without forfeiting any of the other benefits of the school. . . .

----

14. Every school provided by a School Board shall be conducted under the control and management of such Board, in accordance with the following regulations:–

(1) The school shall be a Public Elementary School within the meaning of this Act.

(2) No religious catechism or religious formulary, which is distinctive of any particular denomination, shall be taught in the school.

----

17. Every child attending a school provided by any school board shall pay such weekly fee as may be prescribed by the school board, with the consent of the Education Department, but the school board may from time to time for a renewable period not exceeding six months, remit the whole or any part of such fee in the case of any child when they are of opinion that the parent of such child is unable from poverty to pay the same. . . .

----

74. Every school board may from time to time, with the approval of the Education Department, make byelaws for all or any of the following purposes:

(1) Requiring the parents of children of such age, not less than five years nor more than thirteen years, as may be fixed by the byelaws, to cause such children (unless there is some reasonable excuse) to attend school. . . .

(2) Determining the time during which children are so to attend school. . . .

Statues of the Realm, 33 and 34 Victoria C.75, 1870

(b) The secular case

A School Board for Leeds was elected after a very sharp contest, in November, 1870, and, as was predicted, the cumulative vote secured the victory of the religious bodies over the Liberal Party. . . . The first work of the Board was to provide school accommodation, as the Act directs, for all children of school age, that is, between the ages 5 and 13 – for whom no schools existed. [Out of 47,677 children, 20,000 were found to be unprovided for]. . . . The Board ought at least to have been allowed to provide school accommodation for the 20,000 totally ignorant. These

returns were strongly opposed, as it was found that large districts, amounting to one-fifth of the whole population, were left without a single Board School, on the ground that in some districts –
65 Bramley and Rodley for instance – there was even an excess to a considerable amount by [denominational] schools not yet in existence, *but projected.*

[The author then relates the battle to prevent the fee being raised in the one 'penny fee (per week) school' in Leeds]. The action of the
70 Education Department in raising the fee has made the school a burden to the Rate payers, because it is now only partly filled by children, who attend so irregularly that the educational results are comparatively small, and the children who used to attend are playing about the streets, drifting into poverty and crime. . . . It
75 cannot be said, after such an experience, that the Elementary Education Acts enable the respectable poor to provide education for their children without degradation and loss of self-respect, as, in accordance with the Education Department's instructions and the suggestions of the deputation, poor parents who are willing and
80 able to pay a penny a week are compelled to come before the Board to beg for free schooling. Many will almost starve rather than do this; the wife, as a rule, is sent to make application for the remission of the fees, and before it can be granted she has to prove that the total income of the family, after payment of rent, does not exceed
85 three shillings [15p] per head per week. It sometimes happens from ignorance, as the calculation must be difficult, that she states the income at more than it is, and sometimes less; if the latter, the husband may be prosecuted and fined. . . .

A Sketch of the Elementary Education Question and the Work of the Leeds School Board from 1870 to 1882, Catherine M. Buckton, 1882, pp 8–10, 26, Pamphlets at St Deiniol's Library, Hawarden, 1/F/7

(c) The denominational case

I can quite understand how men who see their own view of a
90 question very clearly, and see nothing else, become intolerant of opposition. Happily unconscious of difficulties themselves, they cannot understand the difficulties of others, and can attribute them only either to weakness or dishonesty. . . . This is natural; but it is unjust. The National Education League, for example, tell us in
95 their latest (and not least characteristic) manifesto, that their scheme of 'united secular and separate religious education' – is the 'only true basis of national education – just to the community, and recognising the claims of all religious denominations'. These gentlemen have a perfect right to think so and to say so; but they
100 have no right either to say or to think that no Dissenter can

honestly and intelligently hold an opposite view. . . .

Modern Non conformity rests, in fact, on a twofold basis – political and religious. As towards the State, it is a claim of freedom; freedom for individuals, freedom for the societies which we call Churches. As towards God, it is an exercise of obedience. The meeting point of these two lies in the fact that we claim from the State freedom to obey God. . . .

[The author is critical of] secular education. That is, education for this world; leaving the next world, if there be one, altogether out of sight. The co-operation between the state and the parent is to be on the principle of limited liability, and the education of the child for anything higher above the earth than he may some day get in a balloon, or further in the future than threescore years and ten, is to be at the parents' sole risk and cost. . . .

The necessity of some government interference with popular education, in the present state of things in England, we are all of us compelled to admit. . . . But whereas some hail this necessary interference as a triumph of progress, and a stride towards higher national organisation and life, others of us lament it as a sign and consequence of national weakness; the dangerous remedy for a fatal disorder. The former party, therefore, would push State education to its utmost systematic completeness; we would lighten the hand of the state as far as possible, and strive yet to preserve what relics of free education can be rescued from the wreck. . . .

Education and Non conformity, A Lecture delivered in East Parade Chapel, Leeds, June 4th 1872, by Eustace R. Conder, pp 4–5, 9, 11, 15, Pamphlets at St Deiniol's Library, Hawarden, 1/J/23

(d) The 1876 Act

1. This Act may be cited as the 'Elementary Education Act, 1876.'

----

4. It shall be the duty of the parent of every child to cause such child to receive efficient elementary instruction in reading, writing and arithmetic, and if such parent fail to perform such duty, he shall be liable to such orders and penalties as are provided by this Act.

----

6. Any person who takes a child into his employment in contravention of this Act (i.e. under 10, or over 10 without a certificate of attendance or proficiency in reading, writing and arithmetic) shall be liable, on summary conviction, to a penalty not exceeding forty shillings [£2].

Statutes of the Realm, 39 and 40 Victoria C.79, 1876

(e) The 1880 Act

An Act to make further provision as to Byelaws respecting the attendance of Children at School under the Elementary Education Acts. . . .

1. This Act may be cited as the Elementary Education Act,
140 1880, and shall be construed as one with the Elementary Education Act, 1876.

2. It shall be the duty of the local authority (within the meaning of the Elementary Education Act, 1876) of every school district in which byelaws respecting the attendance of children at school
145 under section seventy-four of the Elementary Education Act, 1870, are not at the passing of this Act in force, forthwith to make byelaws under that section for such district. . . .

Statutes of the Realm, 43 and 44 Victoria C.23, 1880

Questions

★ *a* By the names of which government ministers are the Education Acts of 1870, 1876 and 1880 (extracts *a, d* and *e*) remembered?

★ *b* By what name is clause 14 of the 1870 Act (extract *a*) known? What controversies lie behind clauses 7 and 14? Were these clauses a satisfactory compromise?

c What elements of the competition between secular and denominational education are revealed by extracts *b* and *c*?

d In what way does extract *b* cast doubt on the adequacy of clause 17 of the 1870 Act for remitting school fees in cases of need?

★ *e* Identify the National Education League (extract *c*, line 94).

f How do the three Acts (extracts *a, d* and *e*) differ in the degree of compulsion to attend elementary school? Where did each Act place the responsibility?

g What more needed to be done after 1876 to establish a compulsory elementary education system accessible to all?

4 Secret voting

For the second time the Ballot Bill formed the main occupation of the Session, and after many checks and delays, caused by the obvious indifference and latent disapproval of the House, Mr. Forster accomplished his unsatisfactory task. The promoters of the
5 Bill candidly admitted that the House of Lords had been justified in previously rejecting an incomplete measure, which was only brought under their consideration at the end of the Session. . . . [Mr. Dacre] ridiculed the trustee notion of the franchise saying that non-electors clearly ought not to dictate for whom the franchise-
10 holder should vote, as otherwise they would be the electors. . . . Mr. Walter, on the other hand, voted against the Ballot, arguing

that its introduction was but preliminary to a new Reform Bill, which would abolish all little boroughs, and boroughs which are really fragments of counties, and enfranchise all country householders. He believed that these boroughs would, under the Bill, be bought wholesale, and that equal electoral districts would soon be inevitable. If the country was not prepared for that, it ought not to pass the Bill. He added, however, that he should oppose it no more. . . .

The first election under the new Act took place in August, at Pontefract, the successful candidate, curiously enough, being Mr. Childers, who solicited re-election on being given a seat in the Cabinet [he had played an active part in the Ballot Bill debate.] He was returned by a vote of 658 to 578, and as the number of registered voters is 1960, more than a third of the constituency abstained from voting. An interesting statement of the working of the Act was sent to the Times by the Mayor of Pontefract. The abolition of the public nomination he regarded as a decided improvement. The excitement and drunkenness which invariably attended the first stage of a contest under the old system were nowhere to be observed on this occasion. The town wore its everyday aspect; hardly any one left his work or business. There was, of course, more bustle on the polling day; but no one was shocked by the familiar scenes of other times. The public-houses were quiet; there was no crowd round the polling-places, and no difficulty in getting to the poll. So much for the external aspect of things. In the mysterious recesses occupied by the returning officer and his deputies the dreaded innovation worked, on the whole, equally well. The illiterates gave some trouble: the time wasted over them was extreme. The average time occupied in taking the votes of those who could read was, however, only from thirty to forty seconds each, and surprise was generally expressed at the simplicity of the process.

Annual Register, 1872, pp 62–73, 74

Questions

a Use this article to reconstruct the arguments used for and against the secret ballot in 1872.

★ *b* When were the further electoral reforms predicted in lines 12–15 brought in?

5 Lowe generates more heat than light

The most amusing part of Mr. Lowe's speech [on the budget of 1871] was his commendation of the stamp on matches, 'not matrimonial engagements', which he proposed to borrow, he said,

from America, as a token of admiration of her finance and goodwill
5 towards herself. The cost of matches is so inappreciable that they are wasted in a most reckless and dangerous way, and are often the cause of most serious fires, as when matches are flung down into areas in which dry straw from unpacked hampers is lying. The Americans, who put ½d [a half penny] on every bundle of 100
10 matches, had realised 400,000 l. a year from the tax. In this country the number manufactured is quite incredible – no less than 560,000,000 *boxes* of wooden matches, and 45,000,000 of wax matches and fusees [large-headed matches]. Mr. Lowe had devised a motto for the new stamp, 'Ex luce lucellum' ('Out of light a little
15 profit'), – a joke not appreciated by the great majority of his hearers, who had evidently forgotten that the diminutive of *lucrum* [profit] contains no *r* – and he thought this would be more suitable to them than the 'rather watery device' of a Noah's ark, which is usually found upon match-boxes. In America the tax was particu-
20 larly easy to collect. . . .

The financial statement was received with blank surprise. Whatever may have been the opinion of his colleagues, Mr. Lowe apparently believed that he had devised an ingenious and satisfactory Budget. His satisfaction was not shared by a single non-official
25 supporter within or without the walls of Parliament. The Match-tax was universally regarded as both a frivolous and a retrograde measure; and a few days afterwards a squalid procession of match-makers from the East End of London to Westminster indicated a risk of popular discontent which it was not desirable to provoke for
30 the sake of a trivial gain. The Government at once yielded either to general opinion or to the demands of the mob, and it was announced that the Match Duty would be struck out of the Budget. But Mr. Lowe and Mr. Gladstone were not warned by their first failure of the imprudence of disregarding the common sentiment of
35 mankind and of offending all who had property to leave or to inherit. Before the resumption of the debate, an intimation was received from a large number of the supporters of Government that they would oppose the increase of the Succession [death] – duty, and accordingly Mr. Gladstone was compelled to announce the
40 withdrawal of the modified Budget, and he proposed in its place the addition of two-pence in the pound to the Income-tax.

Annual Register, 1871, pp 64–5

Questions

a Why might the references to America have been not least among Lowe's gaffes in this case (see Chapter VI, section 2)?

b What damage was done to public perception of the Government's political and financial judgement by this case?

c How far does the article writer betray his political preferences by his emphases and turns of phrase?

6 The rights of labour

(a) Gladstone gives

1. This Act may be cited as 'The Trade Union Act, 1871.'

2. The purposes of any trade union shall not, by reason merely that they are in restraint of trade, be deemed to be unlawful so as to render any member of such trade union liable to criminal prosecution for conspiracy or otherwise.

3. The purposes of any trade union shall not, by reason merely that they are in restraint of trade be unlawful so as to render void or voidable any agreement or trust. . . .

----

6. Any seven or more members of a trade union may by subscribing their names to the rules of the union, and otherwise complying with the provisions of this Act with respect to registry, register such trade union under this Act, provided that if any one of the purposes of such trade union be unlawful such registration shall be void.

----

9. The trustees of any trade union registered under this Act, or any other officer of such trade union who may be authorised so to do by the rules thereof, are hereby empowered to bring or defend, or cause to be brought or defended any action, suit, prosecution, or complaint in any court of law or equity, touching or concerning the property, right, or claim to property of the trade union. . . .

----

11. Every treasurer or other officer of a trade union registered under this Act, at such times as by the rules of such trade union he should render such account as herein-after mentioned, or upon being required so to do, shall render to the trustees of the trade union, or to the members of such trade union, at a meeting of the trade union, a just and true account of all moneys received and paid by him, since he last rendered the like account, and of the balance then remaining in his hands, and of all bonds or securities of such trade union. . . .

Statutes of the Realm, 34 and 35 Victoria C. 31, 1871

(b) Gladstone takes away

An Act to amend the Criminal Law relating to Violence, Threats and Molestation.

Every person who shall do any one or more of the following acts, that is to say,

(1) Use violence to any person or to any property,

(2) Threaten or intimidate any person in such manner as would justify a justice of the peace, on complaint made to him, to bind over the person so threatening or intimidating to keep the peace,

(3) Molest or obstruct any person in manner defined by this section, with a view to coerce such person –

40 (1) Being a master to dismiss or cease to employ any workman, or being a workman to quit any employment or to return work before it is finished;

(2) Being a master not to offer or being a workman not to accept any employment or work;

45 (3) Being a master or workman to belong or not to belong to any temporary or permanent association or combination;

(4) Being a master or workman to pay any fine or penalty imposed by any temporary or permanent association or combination;

50 (5) Being a master to alter the mode of carrying on his business, or the number or description of any person employed by him,

shall be liable to imprisonment with or without hard labour, for a term not exceeding three months. . . .

Statutes of the Realm, 34 and 35 Victoria C.32, 1871

(c) Disraeli restores

55 1. This Act may be cited as the Conspiracy, and Protection of Property Act 1875.

----

3. An agreement or combination by two or more persons to do or procure to be done any act in contemplation or furtherance of a trade dispute between employers and workmen shall not be
60 indictable as a conspiracy if such act committed by one person would not be punishable as a crime.
Nothing in this section shall exempt from punishment any persons guilty of a conspiracy for which a punishment is awarded by any Act of Parliament. Nothing in this section shall affect the law
65 relating to riot, unlawful assembly, breach of the peace, or sedition, or any offence against the State or the Sovereign. . . .

----

17. On and after the commencement of this Act, there shall be repealed;–

I The Act of the session of the thirty-fourth and thirty-
70 fifth years of the reign of her present Majesty, chapter thirty-two, intituled, 'An Act to amend the Criminal Law relating to violence, threats and molestation'. . . .

Statutes of the Realm, 38 and 39 Victoria C.86, 1875

(d) Labour alienated. . .

The result of the Royal Commission in 1867 was. . . the Trade Union Act of 1871, and at last after a further vigorous and

75 persistent agitation carried on in every shape, the Trade Unions gained the full repeal of the penal laws affecting labour combinations. This was not, however, until the year 1875. Thus, in spite of the growing numbers of the Trade Unions and, since 1867, the increasing voting power of the working-classes in the great cities, it 80 took fifty years, from the first act of justice in 1825, to bring about the more complete measure of 1875. . . .

Powerful as the Trade Unions have been, and, indeed, to a certain extent, still are, Trade Unionists are, all, told, but a small fraction of the total working population (at most 600,000 out of a 85 total of 8,000,000). They constitute, in fact, an aristocracy of labour who, in view of the bitter struggle now drawing nearer and nearer, cannot be said to be other than a hindrance to that complete organisation of the proletariat which alone can obtain for the workers their proper control over their own labour. The unfortun- 90 ate sense of superiority which now can be detected, already made itself felt in the Chartist movement. The men who earned thirty shillings or thirty-five shillings [£1.50/£1.75] a week looked down upon the struggle of the less fortunate who earned but fifteen shillings or twelve shillings [75p/60p]. . . . It is this which 95 constitutes the danger of Trade Unionism at the present time to the interests of the mass of the workers. Being also fundamentally unsectarian and unpolitical, they prevent any organised attempt being made by the workers as a class to form a definite party of their own. . . .

100 When the capitalist press congratulates the Trade Unionists on the 'moderation' of their conference, and the capitalist class themselves are good enough to express themselves as 'quite gratified' with the attitude of the two Trade Union members of Parliament [Thomas Burt, Morpeth, and Alexander Macdonald, 105 Stafford; both supported by miners' unions] anyone who understands the real antagonism which exists and must ever exist between the class which provides and the class which trades upon force of labour, can clearly see that the men who pretend to fight the battle of the workers are – possibly with the best intentions – 110 betraying them.

H.M. Hyndman, *The Historical Basis of Socialism in England*, 1883, pp 285–288, 290.

(e) . . . or Labour wooed?

To Lady Chesterfield 29th June 1875

I got to the House of Commons and in good time to witness one of the greatest triumphs that any Government had had in my time – the passing of the Labor Laws amid the enthusiasm of all parties in 115 the House of Commons. The representatives of the artisans, Macdonald, and of the employers – the great employers like Mr.

Tennant of Leeds and others – all sang the same song; and it is not a transient carol. This is the greatest measure since the Short Time Act [is Disraeli referring to the 1874 Factory Act or the legislation 120 of Shaftesbury's era?] and will gain and retain for the Tories the lasting affection of the working classes.

The Letters of Disraeli to Lady Bradford and Lady Chesterfield, ed. Marquis of Zetland, Vol.1, 1929, p 260

Questions

★ *a* Explain the legal cases which led to the 1871 Acts (extracts *a* and *b*).

b Why were these two Acts seen at the time as giving with one hand and taking with the other?

c In what ways were trade unionists' freedom of action enhanced by the 1875 Act (extract *c*)?

★ *d* Identify the viewpoint of the author of extract *d*, and his role in the Labour history of his time.

★ *e* What was 'the first act of justice in 1825' (extract *d*, line 80)? What factors does Hyndman believe secured the trades unions their rights in 1871 and 1875?

★ *f* What developments in the 1880s altered the picture of trade unions that he draws?

g Does Hyndman (extract *d*) or Disraeli (extract *e*) more accurately assess the responses of working men to the 1875 Act?

7 . . . And farewell

(a) An assessment of Gladstone's ministry

Feb. 21 [1874]

The result of the elections was a surprise I believe to most people on both sides. The common opinion was that we should have 20 or 25 majority. The causes of our fall have been so fully written about 5 that there is little for me to say. It is clear that the chief cause was a vague general distrust of the Cabinet and especially of Gladstone. We had exhausted our programme, and quiet men asked, What will Gladstone do next? Will he not seek to recover his popularity by extreme radical measures? It must be admitted that these fears were 10 not altogether groundless. We had really no policy except the financial changes promised by Gladstone: and those measures passed who can tell what our Chief's restless spirit would have turned to?

It would have probably been better if he had brought in his 15 budget before dissolving, but this could not have saved us long. There is evidently a real Conservative reaction; and the other party must have their turn. Of course the tameness of our foreign policy,

Bruce's unlucky management of the beer question, the confusion of the Treasury, Lowe's personal unpopularity, Ayrton's offensive-
20 ness, and other minor causes, helped to precipitate the catastrophe, but we might still have fought on, if the country had not been bent on political repose or inaction. We have had our day, and whatever mistakes we have made, I think our worst enemies must admit that the Gladstone Ministry will fill a not unimportant page in English
25 history. The disestablishment of the Irish Church, the settlement of the Irish Land question, the Education Act, and the abolition of the purchase system and reconstruction of the army are titles to fame which cannot be wrested from us.

Camden 3rd Series Vol. 90 (Camden Miscellary Vol. 21), *A Journal of Events during the Gladstone Ministry 1868–1874 (1st Earl of Kimberley's Journal*), 1958, pp 43–4

Questions

a Which wing of the Liberal party does Kimberley reveal himself as belonging to?

★ *b* Explain Kimberley's references to the actions of Bruce, Lowe and Ayrton.

★ *c* Place Kimberley's comment that 'the other party must have their turn' (line 16) in the context of nineteenth-century political attitudes.

d Do Kimberley's musings support the proposition that elections are lost by governments rather than won by oppositions?

e Can you cite evidence that Kimberley is writing for posterity? Compare his references to Ireland with Chapter VI, section 1.

(b) Rain and waves

The most important news of the week is that the weather has
30 changed. The rain, which seemed so hopelessly persistent, has been at last succeeded in the South of England by bright sunshine and drying winds. The floods have receded from the submerged valleys; the relics of the damaged hay have been collected. . . and the harvest, however late, has become a possible anticipation. . . .
35 Next in interest to the weather is the close of the Parliamentary session and that, too, is now within sight. But the sight has not been reached without a storm to clear the air. Mr. Disraeli, while still refusing to say which of the many minor measures now lingering in various stages he is prepared to sacrifice, announced on
40 Thursday his intention of abandoning the Merchant Shipping Bill – one of the four Bills which on Monday he had placed in front of the Government business. Mr. Plimsoll, excusably excited at this sudden disappointment of all his hopes, burst out into an impassioned appeal to the Minister 'not to consign some thousands

45 of living human beings to a miserable death', and an ardent invective against 'shipowners of murderous tendencies outside the House', who are 'immediately represented in it', and concluded by a vehement declaration with clenched fist and uplifted hand that he would 'unmask the villains who send these sailors to death'. As he
50 had just before given notice of a question he intended to ask about the ownership of certain lost vessels in reference to Mr. Bates, the member for Plymouth, and had threatened similar questions with regard to several other unnamed members, the speaker enquired if he applied the term 'villain' to members of the House, and on his
55 asserting and refusing to withdraw it, Mr. Disraeli had to take the almost unexampled course of moving that the speaker do reprimand the honourable member for Derby. Ultimately, however, Mr. Plimsoll's friends explained that the disappointment had been too much for his over wrought nerves, and that he was really not
60 fully responsible at the moment for his words, and the House very gladly agreed to postpone the motion for a week. Probably by that time Mr. Plimsoll will see the necessity of apologising for conduct which has had the effect of lowering the British House of Commons for the time to the level of an American or French
65 Assembly, and will at the same time find some more parliamentary and not less effective method of expressing the just indignation which the whole country shares with him at this postponement – for it can only be a postponement – of his well-meant and persevering efforts to remedy a grievous wrong.

The Guardian, 28 July 1875 (The weekly periodical, not the Manchester daily).

(c) *Disraeli wrestles with parliamentary business*

70 To Lady Chesterfield — 2Whitehall Gardens
May 7th 1875

MY DEAREST FRIEND,

Don't give up the 'Times' newspaper, for that will deprive you of a great deal of pleasure – among other gratifications the delight of seeing them, in due time, eat all their words and congratulate me
75 upon a triumphant session.

I gave them what they call 'a piece of my mind' when the House met yesterday. Gladstone was furious, although there never was a Leader who treated the House in a more domineering spirit than himself. All I can tell you is that the lecture was not fruitless; the
80 Irish let the Committee close at an early hour and we then made great progress with one of our sanitary Bills, measures which the Liberals particularly wished to prevent passing.

All the trash in the 'Times' about the time wasted by feebly dealing with Privilege and Irish Coercion, I blew into the air by
85 facts which no one could contradict. As it is, we have passed the

Army Exchange Bill, the Artisans' Dwelling Bill which was our chief measure of the session, and in a few days we shall have passed the Irish Bill. . . .

The Letters of Disraeli to Lady Bradford and Lady Chesterfield, ed. Marquis of Zetland, Vol.I, 1929, pp 237–8.

(d) Reflections on Disraeli's fall

To Lady Bradford

Hatfield House
April 2nd 1880

90 I return to town tomorrow and remain there while the dreadful ceremonies are performed. I suppose it may take six weeks – six weeks as disagreeable as can be easily conceived.

Never was so great a discomfiture with a cause so inadequate. I think, so far as I can collect, 'hard Times' was the cry against us.
95 The suffering want a change; no matter what, they are sick of waiting.

The wonderful poll in the City, the numbers at Westminster, the return of Wartley for Sheffield – Greenwich (the only one of the Metropolitan Districts that has yet reached me) prove that the
100 enlightened masses are with us. Had the dissolution been delayed, we should have had to encounter agricultural insurrection as well as our usual foes. The farmers are discontented but they move and conspire slowly. We have been too quick for them. The Farmers' Club have prepared some mischief, but not enough. In a season or
105 two, if fair, the agricultural world will return to its ancient loyalty.

Downing Street
April 8th 1880

I have nothing to say! a most dreary life and labor mine! Winding up a Government as hard work as forming one without any of its excitement. My room is filled with beggars, mournful and indignant, and my desk is covered with letters like a snowstorm.
110 It is the last and the least glorious exercise of power and will be followed, which is the only compensation, by utter neglect and isolation.

The Letters of Disraeli to Lady Bradford and Lady Chesterfield, ed. Marquis of Zetland, Vol.II, 1929, pp 266–7.

Questions

★ *a* With reference to extract *c*, to Chapter IV, section 7, and to your wider reading, identify the sanitary measure referred to and show how its application as a measure of 'permissive legislation' cut across the party lines.

★ *b* What were the background and the sequel to Plimsoll's outburst in the Commons? (extract *b*)?

c What domestic and parliamentary difficulties of Disraeli's ministry are referred to in extracts *a*, *b* and *c*? Can you form any connections between them?

d Were these domestic factors the only reasons for Disraeli's defeat in 1880? See Chapter VI.

VI Foreign and Irish Policies 1868–80

Disraeli never visited Ireland, and Gladstone spent just three weeks there in 1877. Both men were rather more travelled on the continent, although it could be asked to what extent Disraeli's fascination with the East and Gladstone's Homeric studies were practical preparations for unravelling the intricacies of Balkan power politics in the 1870s.

In their compedious works of the 1930s R.W. Seton-Watson and J.L. Hammond chronicled the Eastern and Irish questions respectively, and both painted a picture broadly sympathetic to Gladstone. In this view Gladstone is the would-be liberator of the Irish, hampered only by the extremities of Irish events themselves and the Unionist revolt of 1886. He is the far-sighted champion also of the Balkan nationalities. Disraeli is taken to have no Irish policy, and a dangerous forward foreign policy. Is this interpretation fair?

Disraeli deserves some rehabilitation. He had to wrestle, between 1874 and 1880, with his own poor health, the policy differences with Lords Derby and Salisbury and the Liberal onslaught in speeches and pamphlets. Ironically, though Disraeli enjoyed the acclaim of fashionable and popular opinion in 1878, Gladstone rode to power in 1880 on a reaction against Imperialism. And did the Treaty of Berlin achieve Disraeli's aim of restraining Russia as much as it achieved Gladstone's aim of nationalising the Balkans?

A generous interpretation is that both Gladstone and Disraeli were ahead of their time. Disraeli had a vision of Imperialism, and conceived of a forward policy as the best way to influence powers such as Russia and Turkey. Gladstone's vision embraced the rights of smaller nations, though this vision was selective, applying to the Irish, Bulgarians and Boers but not to the Zulus or Afghans. At the same time he believed in conciliation, arbitration and co-operation between great powers. In this he draws our attention back to the early nineteenth-century 'concert of Europe' and forward to the twentieth century.

The intricacies, tragedies and ironies of Irish history in this period are well documented. Three comments will justify the frequent recurrence of 'the Irish question' in this volume. First, population figures for Ireland and Great Britain, even after the famine, show that Ireland was a much larger part of the United Kingdom, in human terms, in the nineteenth century than in the late twentieth century. Second, electoral arithmetic combined with divisive tendencies within parties made the Irish question of decisive importance in three political crises: 1829–30, 1845–6 and 1885–6. Last, the political aspirations of the Irish always outran the political will even of William Gladstone.

1 The Irish question

(a) Landlords' sensitivities

Farney [Carrickmacross, Co. Monaghan] 1865–1868
. . . I know of nothing more detrimental to the peace and prosperity of a district, than an election for members of Parliament, conducted as such elections generally are in Ireland. The worst
5 passions of the people are aroused to their utmost pitch on both sides, and sectarian animosity and violence seem, demon-like, to possess the whole community. This is not the place to enter upon a discussion as to how all this might be avoided. It is enough to say that it prevails to such a degree as to embitter society on each
10 occasion of its recurrence, so that we have scarcely had time to recover from the angry feelings of one election before another springs into its place.

I am well aware of the unhappy position of affairs in Ireland which renders these unfortunate differences almost natural and
15 indigenous to the soil. The owners of landed property are in general Protestants. The occupiers are in general Roman Catholics. And in many of the great questions of the day which come before Parliament, and to which the Country representatives are called on to pledge themselves, the interests of the owners and those of the
20 occupiers are considered by each class to be antagonistic.

The landed proprietor feels that in the selection of a Member of Parliament he has only one vote; and no matter how large his interest or stake in the country may be he has *constitutionally* nothing to throw into the scale against those who would overturn
25 the most cherished institutions of the realm, except this unit vote. He sees with ill-suppressed indignation that the smallest holder and most ignorant peasant on his estate has by law the same power as himself, and, if uninfluenced by him, will probably make use of it in overturning all that he he has been accustomed to hold sacred.
30 The tenant again, on his side, maintains that if he pays his rent, cultivates his farm, and fulfils his other engagements with his landlord, the latter has no right to make any further demand upon

him, and, backed by his priest, he resists all interference with his vote.

W. Steuart Trench (Land Agent in Ireland to the Marquis of Lansdowne, the Marquis of Bath and Lord Digby), *Realities of Irish Life*, 1868, pp 347–8

Questions

a How adequately do these two extracts describe the 'Irish question'?

b In what ways are their biases and points of view revealed?

(b) Tenants' tribulations

35 England has been left in possession not only of the soil of Ireland, with all that grows and lives thereon, to her own use, but in possession of the world's ear also. She may pour into it what tale she will: and all mankind will believe her.

Success confers every right in this enlightened age; wherein, for 40 the first time, it has come to be admitted and proclaimed in set terms, that Success is Right, and Defeat is Wrong. If I profess myself a disbeliver in this gospel, the enlightened age will only smile, and say, 'the defeated always are'. Britain being in possession of the floor, any hostile comment upon her way of 45 telling our story is an unmannerly interruption; nay, is nothing short of an Irish *howl*. . . .

For not one instant did the warfare cease upon farming Celts. In 1843, 'Government' issued a notable commission; that is, appointed a few landlords, with Lord Devon at their head, to go 50 through Ireland, collect evidence, and report on the best means (not of destroying the Irish enemy – official documents do not use so harsh language, but) of ameliorating the relations of landlord and tenant in Ireland. On this commission O'Connell observed that it was 'a jury of butchers trying a sheep for his life', and said many 55 other good things both merry and bitter, as was his wont; but the Devon Commission travelled and reported; and its Report has been the Gospel of Irish Landlords and British Statesmen ever since.

Three sentences of their performance will show the drift of it. Speaking of 'Tenant Right' (a kind of unwritten law whereby 60 tenants in the north were secure from ejectment from their farms while they paid their rent, a custom many ages old, and analogous to the customs of farmers all over Europe), these commissioners reported 'that they foresaw some dangers to the just rights of property from the unlimited allowance of this tenant-right'. On the 65 propriety of consolidating farms (that is, destroying many small farmers to set up one large one), the Commissioners say, 'when it is seen in the evidence, and in the return of the size of farm, how minute these holdings are, it cannot be denied that such a step is *absolutely necessary.*'

70 But the most remarkable sentence occurs in Lord Devon's 'Digest of the Evidence', page 399:

'We find that there are at present 326,084 occupiers of land (more than one-third of the total number returned in Ireland), whose holdings vary from seven acres to less than one acre; and are, 75 therefore, inadequate to support the families residing upon them. In the same table, No. 95, page 564, *the calculation is put forward*, showing that the consolidation of these small holdings up to eight acres, would require the *removal* of about 192,368 families.'–

That is, the killing of a million of persons. Little did the 80 Commissioners hope then, that in four years, British policy, with the famine to aid, would succeed in killing fully two millions, and forcing nearly another million to flee the country.

John Mitchel, *Jail Journal, or, Five Years in British Prisons*, 1868, pp 1, 17–18

(c) The Fenians

While the virulent distemper of the Fenian conspiracy manifested in former years evinced in the present no abatement, the insurrection-85 ary spirit now broke out in a new quarter, and assumed a still more alarming aspect. In 1865–6, its principal explosions took place on Irish ground – in 1867 the insurgents conceived the idea of producing a stronger impression of their capacity for mischief by extending their operations to this country, and caused the peaceable 90 inhabitants of English towns to tremble for the safety of their homes and families.

In the month of February, within a few days after the Ministers had announced the early restoration of the Habeas Corpus to Ireland, a band of Conspirators, directed by former officers of the 95 American army, planned a surprise of the Arsenal at Chester. . . . Soon after the failure of the intended attack on Chester, the Fenian leaders commenced in different parts of Ireland an insurrection which proved completely abortive. In the neighbourhood of Dublin, in Kerry, and at Drogheda, half-armed bodies assembled 100 early in March, with the obvious purpose of compelling the Government to dissipate its military force. The army was rapidly disposed so as to crush any attempt at rebellion, but its services were scarcely needed. The admirable conduct of the police justified the confidence which had been habitually reposed in the loyalty and 105 courage of a purely Irish force. . . . In the trials which followed, the juries, as in the previous year, discharged their duties with impartial firmness, proving that the middle class was still generally exempt from the contagion of treason [The Government commuted the death sentence on the rebel leaders and imprisoned them

110 in England]. . . . The attack on the prison-van at Manchester, the rescue of the Fenian prisoners, and the murder of the brave officer of police who died in defence of his post of duty, proved that the audacity of the rebels was carried to a pitch that defied all consequences, and hesitated at no sacrifice which might further
115 their treasonable objects. . . . [Subsequently] an attempt, which happily proved abortive, to deliver some of their confederates from prison [at Clerkenwell], resulted in a heavy sacrifice of innocent lives, and the infliction of a great amount of suffering and misery upon a number of helpless and inoffensive persons.
120 Although the Clerkenwell outrage differed only in degree from the Manchester murder, promiscuous slaughter of the unoffending occupiers of a back lane in London struck the popular imagination more forcibly than a revolver fired at a constable.

Annual Register, 1867, pp 199–200

Questions

- ★ *a* Outline the American background to Fenianism, alluded to in line 95.
- *b* What instances of loyalism in Ireland does the extract note?
- ★ *c* What difficulties did the Governments of the late 1860s have in establishing the balance between coercion and conciliation in Ireland? Draw material from the extract to support your answer.

(d) Church and land reform

July 22 [1869]. All is settled [the Irish Church Bill]. Ld. Cairns, it
125 seems, wrote a note to Granville this morning offering to discuss with him the terms of a compromise. They met at the Colonial Office in the afternoon, and with the help of the Irish Attorney General, who was the only other person present at the interview, came to an arrangement. Cairns' speech in the House announcing
130 the compromise was in excellent taste, at once dexterous and firm. Salisbury on the other hand could not conceal his vexation. His speech was waspish and ineffective. Disraeli is said, probably with truth, to have been the prime mover in this settlement of the question, being persuaded that as long as it remained open the
135 Liberal majority could not be broken.
Feb. 21 [1870]. The undiscriminating praise with which the Land Bill was received begins to cool down. In Ireland, as I expected, there is much disappointment. No measure, not robbing the Landlords of their property would satisfy the tenant right party.
140 Indeed no measures of any kind can satisfy the Irish: the utmost they can do is to lay the basis for a gradual improvement. Gladstone now lives in the happy delusion that his policy will

produce a speedy change in the temper of the Irish towards this country. He will soon find out his mistake.

145 March 2 [1870]. A strong feeling of dissatisfaction is growing up at the neglect of the Government to take more stringent measures for the repression of the agrarian crime which has reached a fearful height in some of the Irish countries, principally in Westmeath & Mayo.

Camden 3rd Series Vol. 90 (Camden Miscellany Vol. 21), *A Journal of Events during the Gladstone Ministry 1864–1874 (1st Earl of Kimberley's Journal)*, 1958, pp 7, 11, 12

Questions

★ *a* What offices did Kimberley hold in Gladstone's first ministry?

★ *b* What was the nature of the compromise (line 126) by which the House of Lords was persuaded to pass the Irish Church Act?

c Comment on Disraeli's tactics (lines 132–135).

d Why was the Irish Land Act so much less controversial at Westminster than the Irish Land Act?

e How perceptive is Kimberley's assessment of the Irish Land Act?

(e) The Land League

150 The harvest of 1877 . . . was disastrous. . . . The harvest of 1878 was also a failure. . . . In the winter of 1878 the Irish farmers woke up to the terrible fact that, on the hazard of yet another crop, that of 1879, their very existence hung. . . . Now, indeed, they bitterly realised that the Land Act of 1870 was but a 'monument of good

155 intentions'. It had been wholly impotent to protect them from the dexterous and relentless confiscation wrought by a yearly twist of the rent-screw. . . .

The winter months of 1878–79 went through amidst such crowding signs of fear and trouble, when, towards the end of

160 April, 1879, a call went round amongst the farmers of West Mayo to assemble on the 28th of the month at Irishtown to consider the position of affairs. This meeting was the work of a man whose name . . . must ever be associated with the overthrow of feudal landlordism in Ireland – Michael Davitt [Davitt's family had

165 experienced eviction and emigration to Lancashire. By missing a train he was prevented from attending the Irishtown rally].

. . . How would the Home Rulers like to see a movement pushed to the front that might, for a time at all events, hide away their own? How would the remnants of the Fenian battalions –

170 broken, disrupted, scattered, weakened, but not destroyed – take to a course of action which was to be open and above-board, avoiding violence and illegality, and working only by the ordinary

modes of political warfare? Above all – and this seemed his greatest obstacle – how would the public men, the Catholic clergy, and the
175 existing Tenant-Right organisations . . . receive a project, the first principle of which was to decry and contemn as utterly inadequate 'the Three F's', till now the maximum of the tenants' demands? [Parnell is converted to the cause of the Irish Land movement].

On the 21st October [1879], in response to a circular from him, a
180 meeting was held in Dublin of tenant-farmer delegates and friends, whereat was formed 'The Irish National Land League'. . . .

[Starvation, rent demands and evictions begin to take a grip.] As Mr. Gladstone once well expressed it, they fell like 'snowflakes' on the districts least able to pay; processes for rent that the landlords
185 well knew the land had not earned. At a place called Carraroe, in Connemara, on the 5th of January, 1880, bailiffs made their appearance with sheaves of the documents, escorted by a detachment of armed police. The wretched peasants took alarm, and, assembling in haste, confronted the invading force. The women –
190 most of the male inhabitants happened to be away harvesting in England at the time [in January? – author] – exhibited a fierce daring absolutely without precedent till then in these agrarian affrays. They flung themselves before the bayonets and barred the way to the threatened homesteads. A bloody conflict ensued, the
195 police freely using their arms, and the women displaying utter recklessness of life. In the result the people were victorious. The invaders had to retreat, leaving the processes unserved.

This was the Lexington of the agrarian revolution in Ireland. From that day forth the whole procedure of eviction, step by step,
200 inch by inch, was contested, obstructed, resisted. The women of Carraroe struck the first blow in the war against Rent.

A.M. Sullivan (Irish Nationalist MP), *New Ireland, Political Sketches and Personal Reminiscences of Thirty Years of Irish Public Life*, 7th edition, 1882, pp 430, 431, 434, 438, 445

Questions

a By Sullivan's account, where in the spectrum of Irish political organisations did the Land League lie?

★ *b* To what legislative measure did the campaign for 'the three Fs' lead? Why, according to the evidence in this extract, would 'the three Fs' not be an adequate solution to the Land problem?

★ *c* How did the Land League campaign of resistance develop after the Carraroe episode?

d What examples occur in the extract of employment opportunities for Irish people in England?

★ *e* Much attention has been paid to Gladstone's Irish policy, but this extract focuses on the years of Disraeli's premiership. Did Disraeli have an Irish policy?

2 The Alabama award

Mr. G. to Lord Granville, Hawarden Castle Jan. 14, [18]72

I very decidedly agree with you that we ought not to go out of the line of proceeding laid down in the Alabama case for the purpose of protesting. I have not seen the American case yet. But it looks to 5 me as if, supposing it to be as it is described, all the bunkum and irrelevant trash might be handled in some degree as 'Americanism' due to want of knowledge of the world and of European manners. We cannot in *propriâ personâ* [in our own person] go far in this line: but I think much might perhaps be made of it in a pamphlet or 10 some other unofficial medium, through which we might retaliate a little, show up their method of working foreign politics for home purposes, and allow that it was too much to expect from the President [Ulysses S. Grant], who has got to be re-elected, with Sumner for an enemy, altogether to avoid reproducing Sumner's 15 notorious speech [in the Senate, causing the rejection of the 'Alabama' settlement terms], although he must have known it could only do mischief to his case, if it did *anything*, before a Tribunal of Arbitrators.

Lord Granville to Mr. Gladstone

20 This 3 000 000 £ & something more award will not be popular here – and will create an angry debate in each house. If the Arbitrators are right as to the Alabama, and their unanimity ought to be a presumption in their favor, I doubt whether they are wrong about the Florida and the Shenandoah although the last raises some 25 awkward questions as to our Colonial liabilities. I see nothing to make me doubt the perfect good faith of the Italian and Brazilian. [Sir Alexander] Cockburn has been a bad Arbitrator for us. [Charles] Adams [American arbitrator] most judicious and on the whole not unfair considering his position.

The Political Correspondence of Mr. Gladstone and Lord Granville 1868–1876, ed. Agatha Ramm, Camden 3rd Series Vol. 82, pp 298–9, 342

Questions

★ *a* Outline the background of the 'Alabama' case. Why was compensation due to the USA because of the actions of 'Alabama', 'Florida' and 'Shenandoah'?

b To what do Granville and Gladstone attribute the adverse decision of the arbitrators?

★ *c* What were the repercussions at home of the 'Alabama' award?

3 Russia and the Black Sea

Nov. 10 [1870]. We have a most unpleasant matter to deal with in the Russian repudiation of the articles of the Treaty of Paris relating to the Black Sea. The cool insolence and dishonesty of this proceeding are just what might be expected from Prince Gortchacov in whose hands the Czar is a mere puppet. Unfortunately in the present state of Europe we can do nothing but protest. My theory of the situation is this – Bismarck and Gortchacov had an understanding when the war broke out. Russia engaged to keep Austria in check in return for which Russia was to favour Russia's design to set aside the Treaty of Paris. When France collapsed, Gortchacov was afraid that Bismarck would play the same trick as he played France after Sadowa. Seeing however that the Russians were unexpectedly held at bay by Paris he seized the opportunity much to the annoyance of Bismarck to take a decisive step as to the Black Sea. Bismarck of course does not intend to quarrel with Russia, the consequence of which might be that we might find it advisable to attempt to give some aid to France. He therefore temporizes and will try to smooth the matter down.

Camden 3rd Series Vol. 90 *(1st Earl of Kimberley's Journal)*, op. cit., p 19

Questions

★ *a* Explain the references to the Treaty of Paris (lines 2 and 10) and Sadowa (line 12).

★ *b* According to Kimberley, is it Bismarck or Gortchacov who takes the initiative in the repudiation of the Black Sea clauses? Does this account agree with the evidence of your wider reading?

4 The Suez Canal shares

Hickleton [near Doncaster], Nov. 28 [18]75

Mr. G[ladstone] to Lord Granville

I am glad to think you were not alone at Walmer [Kent] when the startling news arrived about the purchase of the Khedive's interest in the Suez Canal. We reckon that Cardwell was with you. But you may like to know how it strikes other friends, and even what are the sentiments of a disembodied spirit like myself.

Amid the conflicting statements that have appeared, I find the meeting point of them all in the version which seems as follows.

a. The purchase is immediate

b. The payment is immediate

c. For a term of years the Khedive guarantees 5 per cent upon the money: after which we get the Dividend yielded by the concern.

d. In some manner it is subject to the consent of Parliament; and I imagine they are hardly in a condition to pay the four millions themselves outright, though some finance-agent may do it on the strength of the pledge to apply to parliament.

e. There is no present sign of an intention to summon the two
20 Houses for the purpose.

A storm of approbation seems to swell, almost to rage, on every side.

I write in mild language, out of respect, such respect as is due, to the sense of what seems an overwhelming majority. But my
25 opinion on the imperfect information before me is this. If the thing had been done in Concert with the other Powers, it is an act of folly, fraught with future embarrassment. If without such concert, it is an act of folly fraught also with present danger.

I am aware of no cause that could warrant or excuse it, except its
30 being necessary to prevent the closing of the Canal. But that cause I apprehend could not possibly exist. The closing of the London and North Western [Railway] would be about as probable. . . .

The Political Correspondence of Mr. Gladstone and Lord Granville 1868–1876, ed. Agatha Ramm, Camden 3rd Series Vol. 82, pp 473–4

Questions

★ *a* Identify the Khedive. Why did he sell his shares in the Suez Canal?

b Why does Gladstone refer to himself as 'a disembodied Spirit' (line 7)?

c On what grounds does Gladstone criticise the purchase?

★ *d* How was the purchase financed?

e In what ways does this extract reveal Gladstone to be out of step, and Disraeli in step, with popular opinion?

5 The Question of the East

(a) Gladstone opens

In the discussion of this great and sad subject [the Bulgarian atrocities] the attitude and the proceedings of the British Government cannot possibly be left out of view. Indeed, the topic is, from the nature of the case, so prominent, and from the acts done, so
5 peculiar, that I can hardly be excused from stating in express and decided terms what appear to me its grave errors. . . . They have not understood the rights and duties, in regard to the subjects, and particularly the Christian Subjects, of Turkey, which inseparably attach to this country in consequence of the Crimean War, and of
10 the Treaty of Paris, in 1856. They have been remiss when they ought to have been active; namely, in efforts to compose the Eastern revolts, by making provision against the terrible misgov-

ernment which provoked them. They have been active, where they ought to have been circumspect and guarded – It is a grave change, 15 which cannot be withheld, that they have given to a maritime measure of humane precaution the character of a military demonstration in support of the Turkish Government. . . .

Down to this date what we have to observe is–

First. The deplorable inefficiency of the arrangements of the 20 Government for receiving information.

Secondly. The yet more deplorable tardiness of the means, adopted under Parliamentary pressure, for enlarging their store of knowledge.

Thirdly. The effect of the answers of the Prime Minister, from 25 which it could not but be collected, by Parliament and the public,

a. That the responsibility lay in the first instance with certain 'invaders of Bulgaria'.

b. That the deplorable atrocities, which had occurred, were fairly divided, and were such as were incidental to wars 'between 30 certain *races*'. . . .

c. While the Bulgarians were thus loaded with an even share of responsibility for the 'atrocities', we were given to understand that the Turkish Government, and its authorized agents, appeared to be no parties to them.

35 d. That the 'Scenes', that is, as is now demonstrated, the wholesale murders, rapes, tortures, burnings, and the whole devilish enginery of crime, 'were to be mitigated and softened as much as possible'. . . . [the pamphlet proceeds to its climax in the famous 'bag and baggage' passage].

W.E. Gladstone, *Bulgarian Horrors and the Question of the East*, 1876, pp 16–17, 24–25

(b) Disraeli responds

Hughenden
40 To Lady Chesterfield August 31st 1876

Here there is only one business and that is one I cannot write about. If we don't get peace it will be owing, in the slight degree, to our enlightened public who, as usual, have fallen into the Russian trap, and denouncing 'Bulgarian atrocities', call for the expulsion of 45 the Turks from Europe, which would lead to another Thirty Years' war.

Hughenden Manor
To Lady Bradford September 1st 1876

. . . Everything has gone against us – but nothing so much as the 'Bulgarian atrocities' which have changed the bent of opinion in 50 England as regards Turkey and which are worked not merely by enthusiasts, but of course by the Opposition and by Russia's agents, though the Government have no more to do with the 'atrocities' than the man in the moon. Gortchakoff is, of course, in the seventh heaven and smiles while he proposes an armistice of 55 three months – equivalent to renewed war with renovated energies.

Hughenden Manor
To Lady Bradford September 5th 1876

. . . Gladstone 'who had retired from public life', can't resist the first opportunity and is going to declaim at Blackheath – having 60 preliminarily given the cue to public opinion in a pamphlet. I wonder what Hartington thinks of all this activity? He is quietly killing grouse at Bolton Abbey, and this very morning sent me four brace. Good fellow!

The state of affairs is not one very favourable to the nervous 65 system – but mine is not yet shaken.

Alway yours
B.

The Letters of Disraeli to Lady Bradford and Lady Chesterfield, ed. Marquis of Zetland, Vol. II, 1929, pp 69–71

(c) Tories attacked

Somerleaze [Wells, Somerset]
To Miss Edith Thompson December 24th 1876

. . . I have sent you my Manchester speech; of the full report of the Conference they have sent me only one; so you may spend a shilling in buying what Gladstone and I really said. How the Jews, 70 Turks, and Tories do lie! See, even those whom one looked on as honest men are carried away by their dissimulation. I had more anonymous letters of abuse yesterday than I ever had in one day before. But the more the merrier; it shows that they are hard hit. I have not forgotten what S.G. Selwyn of Milton Clevedon said to 75 me in 1868: 'I speak of you as contemptible, because I know that you are formidable'. Still they need not lie, but I suppose with the Jew at their head they really cannot help it. The words 'perish India' were not only never said, but were not even reported – at least not in *Times, Daily News, Daily Telegraph,* or *Standard*; they are pure 80 invention. Yet I get abusive letters charging me with lying in saying that I did not say them. . . .

The St. James' Hall Conference was a wonderful sight – I did not twenty years back expect to hear some thousands of Englishmen cheering every word in favour of Russia. Even Gladstone fell dead 85 when he made the slightest hint the other way. It is perfectly true that my reception was next to Gladstone's. The sniggering only shows what a move it was.

All this sadly tells against work [as a History scholar and writer].

The Life and Letters of Edward A. Freeman, ed. W.R.W. Stephens, Vol. II, 1895, pp 143–4

(d) Gladstone answered

[The underlinings, and the exclamation marks after 'unheard' (line 107), were added in pencil, probably by Gladstone, to the copy at St. Deiniol's Library, Hawarden, Pamphlets 11/A/4].

Bismallah! – In the name of the Prophet I take up my pen in
90 defence of my race and people, and may Allah, the Lord of all, direct my efforts towards success in the self-appointed task and take in hand, and through me be the means of enlightening the great and just English nation. . . .

The English nation boasts of its love for 'fair play', and in this
95 nineteenth century I cannot believe that it would willingly allow itself to be biassed by religious considerations when judging between man and man, or nation and nation. The indictment against us brought by Russia in the first instance, warmly supported by the eloquent writings and speeches of some of your
100 ablest men, is that the Osmanli as a nation is worn out and effete. . . .

There are some amongst you . . . who do justice to the Osmanli as a nation, whilst condemning its Government; and it is in support of their voices, now beginning to obtain some hearing, that I write
105 this present address. Their voices were stifled in the beginning by the clamour raised against us on account of the Bulgarian atrocities . . . our judges were biassed, and we were sentenced <u>unheard!!</u> . . . [Our critics] were first in the field, and could write their impressions on a clear surface.
110 I am not coming forward as an apologist for the crimes committed in the suppression of the Bulgarian rebellion. <u>Willingly would I erase all recollection of them from the public mind</u>; but as that is impossible, and they were made the groundwork for the many changes brought against us showing our unfitness to rule in
115 Europe, I cannot remain altogether silent. I will ask whether your Consular reports do not fully show that Russia, ever since the Crimean War, has been actively employed, through her many agents, in stirring up discontent in the Provinces? . . . With such clear proof as the world has unfortunately seen of late of the real
120 nature of the Bulgarian, his capabilities for crime and cruel deeds, will any one now deny the truth of the evidence as to the atrocities being first committed by them? . . .

The English are a great and generous nation much more impulsive than generally imagined. It is easily led by those who

125 know how to humour its prejudices and, unfortunately for us, there was a party in England seeking an opportunity for returning to power. The Government of Lord Beaconsfield was true to the traditional policy of England. . . . Fiercely assailed, the Government was attacked on all sides by party clamour, like a ship in the
130 storm, was obliged for a time to lower its sails and run before the blast, but ever at the helm the stout-hearted Beaconsfield stood watching for the chance to bring the good ship back to her course, and his name has become a household name in Turkey. . . .

Hadji Achmet Effendi, *The Cloud on the Crescent, A word for the Turks, by one of themselves, in answer to Mr. Gladstone*, 1878, pp 3, 6–9, Pamphlets at St Deiniol's Library, Hawarden, 11/A/4

(e) Liberal ditties. . .

SONG OF THE DAY: WILL GLADSTONE
[To the tune of 'When Johnny comes marching home'?]

1. We'll have Will Gladstone back again, hurrah! hurrah!
135 We'll make him take the helm again! hurrah! hurrah!
And rid we'll be of the boasting crew
Whose Tory trump so loudly blew,
For WILL was ever brave and true, hurrah! hurrah! hurrah!

2. And where shall Dizzy go my boys? ha ha! ha ha!
140 Why, Turkey lads, will be his choice; ha ha! ha ha!
And the coat-of-arms he sports in Burke
Shall bear the Moslem's bloody dirk;
Be sure the Turk, for his dirty work, will make him a Pacha!

3. And where shall the Earl of Derby go? ha ha! ha ha!
145 Oh! back again, to the 'status quo;' ha ha, ha ha!
From whence he came, with a mighty name
For wisdom, but it's all the same,
We've done with him and his Eastern game! hurrah! hurrah! hurrah!
150 [etcetera!]

Tory Sympathy with Turkish Barbarities, Pamphlets at St. Deiniol's Library, Hawarden, GX/E/3

(f) . . . and Tory doggerel

Young England's Alphabet of the War. By J.H.

A is atrocities got up by Russia
As pretexts to fall upon Turkey, and crush her.
B is Bulgaria's base, brutal work;
155 where cold-blooded Russia outrivals the Turk.
C Constantinople, the card of old Nick,

And Aleck his son: but we'll soon trump their *trick!*
D stands for Dardanelles: Russians are clever,
And wish they may get 'em: but England says, Never!
160 E stands for England, cajoled by a faction,
Till almost too late to take resolute action.
F stands for Folly, by Feeling unmanned;
And Factions Fatuity rife in the Land.
G stands for Gladstone; if now he is glad,
165 His heart must be stone; or the man *must* be mad!
[etcetera!]

The Crisis, or Gladstonism Unmasked, A series of satires for the times, ed. Tom Brown Jun., Bristol, 1876, p 18, Pamphlets at St. Deiniol's Library, Hawarden, GX/B/5

Questions

- *a* Gather and analyse the references to Britain's past relations with Russia in extracts *a, c* and *d*.
- *b* Which is the main object of Gladstone's attack (extract *a*): the Turkish Government or the British?
- ★ *c* Explain Gladstone's references to a 'maritime measure of humane precaution' (extract *a*, line 15).
- *d* Why can Disraeli not talk about the 'business' of the day (extract *b*, line 41)?
- ★ *e* Why would the expulsion of the Turks from Europe lead to another 30 years' war? (extract *b*, line 45)?
- *f* What is the significance of Disraeli's placing 'atrocities' in quotation marks (extract *b*, line 44)?
- ★ *g* Identify Gortchacov (extract *b*, line 53). Why is he 'in the seventh heaven'?
- *h* Why might Hartington not be wholly in support of Gladstone's stand in this affair?
- *j* At what points does Freeman (extract *c*) claim to have been misrepresented?
- *k* How does Hadji Achmet (extract *d*) woo the English by references to their national characteristics? Is he wholly complimentary?
- *l* In what respects does he concede the case against Turkey?
- *m* What responsibility does he place on the Bulgarians?
- *n* Was Lord Beaconsfield 'true to the traditional policy of England' (extract *d*, line 127)?
- *p* If the pencil annotations in extract *d* are Gladstone's, what do his reactions to the pamphlet seem to have been?
- *q* What insights into the political methods and media of the 1870s are provided by these extracts? In particular what baser elements of political opinion are evident in extracts *c, e* and *f*?
- ★ *r* By what policies and actions was Disraeli enabled to regain the initiative in the Eastern Question from Gladstone by 1878?

6 The Midlothian campaign

(a) Dangers of a forward policy

[Gladstone's first Midlothian speech, Music Hall, George Street, Edinburgh]

. . . But what has been the course of things for the last three years? . . . We have got an annexation of territory . . . in the Fiji
5 Islands, of which I won't speak, because I don't consider the Government is censurable for that act . . . . They have annexed in Africa the Transvaal territory, inhabited by a free European, Christian, republican community, which they have thought proper to bring within the limits of a monarchy, although out of 8000
10 persons in that republic qualified to vote upon the subject, we are told, and I have never seen the statement officially contradicted, that 6500 protested against it . . . . We have made war on the Zulus. We have therefore become responsible for their territory; and not only this, but we are now, as it appears from the latest
15 advices, about to make war on a chief lying to the northward of the Zulus; and Sir Bartle Frere, who was the great authority for the proceedings of the Government in Afghanistan, has announced in South Africa that it will be necessary for us to extend our dominions until we reach the Portuguese frontier to the north. . . .
20 In Europe we have annexed the island of Cyprus. . . . We have assumed jointly with France the virtual government of Egypt. . . . We then, gentlemen, have undertaken to make ourselves responsible for the good government of Turkey in Asia. . . . Besides governing it well, we have undertaken to defend the Armenian
25 frontier of Turkey against Russia. . . .

Well, and as if that were not enough, we have, by the most wanton invasion of Afghanistan, broken that country into pieces, made it a miserable ruin, destroyed whatever there was in it of peace and order, caused it to be added to the anarchies of the
30 Eastern world, and we have become responsible for the management of the millions of warlike but very partially civilised people whom it contains. . . .

I really have but one great anxiety. This is a self-governing country. Let us bring home to the minds of the people the state of
35 the facts they have to deal with, and in Heaven's name let them determine whether or not this is the way in which they like to be governed. . . .

W.E. Gladstone, *Political Speeches in Scotland,* November and December 1879, Pub. 1880, pp 48–50

(b) Gladstone's progress

HAWARDEN, December 8th–14th 1879. I went to Hawarden Tuesday, arriving there the day after the Gladstones, who were

40 received with frantic enthusiasm at Chester, after the memorable Midlothian campaign. It has been one long outburst of welcome and one long triumph; yet the Conservatives still talk of winning. Uncle W. has poured out 6 magnificent speeches besides a very noble Rectorial address at Glasgow! and endless little addresses
45 delivered bare-headed in the keen frosty weather; and here he is as fresh as paint. Not so poor auntie [Mrs. Gladstone]; she had to take to her bed Wednesday with a bad chill, which developed into erysipelas in her face. . . . [She describes the social round] the Great Man all the while interesting and delightful *beyond*. For the 1st
50 time, I deliberately believe, in my recollections, he seems a little *personally* elated! It has always hitherto been the cause, or the moment, or the circumstances, or *something* that he thinks he is the mere mouthpiece of; but this unheard-of enthusiasm for his name, in his own country. . . and after the long time of abuse and loss of
55 influence, has deeply moved him. . . .

The Diary of Lady Frederick Cavendish, ed. John Bailey, Vol. II, 1927, pp 240–1

(c) Forward policy defended

Sir,

In the course of a political tour in Scotland in 1879 you introduced my name in some of your many speeches as one of the principal instigators of a foreign policy, which you denounced as
60 wicked and aggressive, as depraving the morality, and ruining the finances, of England.

These speeches, I need hardly say, produced an immense effect on public opinion, both in England and in the distant colony where I was then on duty [Cape Colony].

65 [Frere announces his intention of clearing himself and his government of accusations of injustice and aggression]. . . . He [Gladstone] will. . . find that for close on a quarter of a century I have persistently urged on the Government of India, and through it, on the Government of England, presided over for a great
70 portion of that time by Mr. Gladstone himself, the only policy which, as later events have shown, could have *prevented* the necessity for any military advance into Afghanistan.

When Lord Canning was Viceroy of India, an opportunity offered for restoring more friendly relations with the Afghans. . . .
75 I was then senior member of Lord Canning's Council, and pressed as strongly as I could on the viceroy, and not for the first time, that advantage should be taken of. . . expressions of Afghan good will to restore more cordial relations with the Afghan Government and Sirdars [military chiefs]. . . . This view . . . was, I believe, laid
80 before Her Majesty's Government in England, of which Mr.

Gladstone was then, I think, a member [Frere had left India in 1867].

The result was the expression to Lord Canning of a very strong opinion (i.e. of the English Cabinet) that we should have as few
85 relations as possible, whether friendly or otherwise, with the Afghans. . . .

Does [Mr Gladstone] still think that, if we had gone on shutting our eyes and turning our backs on the Afghans, we should have improved their feelings towards us, or kept the Russians further
90 from the Indus?. . .

There are obvious reasons why I cannot at present follow Mr. Gladstone throughout his denunciations of the Zulu war. . . . [Frere challenges Gladstone with the following points:]

(1) That the numbers and force of the Zulu army have been
95 proved by inexorable facts to have been greater, and their organization more perfect than my highest official estimate before Lord Chelmsford's first advance.

(2) That in the judgement of all military authorities, both before the war and since, it was absolutely impossible for Lord Chelm-
100 sford's force, acting on the defensive, within the Natal boundary, to prevent a Zulu impi from entering Natal, and repeating the same indiscriminate slaughter of all ages and sexes which they boast of having effected in Natal. . . forty years ago, and . . . within the last two years.

105 These facts seem to me to prove that I did not over estimate the Zulu danger . . . . Would Mr. Gladstone believe any civilized monarch on the earth, if he said that such a universal enrolment and training of the whole male population was not intended to be used for any military purpose?

110 If he would not believe such assertion made by a European Emperor, how can he attach any weight to it when volunteered, not by, but for, a barbarian Chief, whose own boast is that he acknowledges no superior, and that unrestrained power to shed blood is a national necessity, without which the Zulus could not exist as a nation?

Sir Bartle Frere, *Afghanistan and South Africa, A letter to the Right Hon. W.E. Gladstone, M.P., regarding portions of his Midlothian speeches,* 1881, pp 5, 6, 10–14, Pamphlets at St. Deiniol's Library, Hawarden, GX/H/1

Questions

a Where in extracts *a* and *b* are hints made about an impending election?

b What elements of the Midlothian campaign represent novel political methods?

c What are the 'obvious reasons' why (Frere) cannot at present follow Mr. Gladstone throughout his denunciations of the Zulu war' (extract *c*, lines 91–92)?

★ *d* Identify the Zulu chief to whom Frere refers (extract *c*). What light do extracts *a* and *c* shed on the triangular conflict between Zulus, Boers and British?

★ *e* From the evidence of extracts *a* and *c*, and from your wider study, assess to what extent Disraeli had a forward imperial 'policy', and to what extent British forces were drawn or propelled forward by circumstances in Africa and Asia.

VII Disraeli and Gladstone: Personalities and Personal Relationships

The close study of personalities in History has two main purposes. The first is to challenge the superficial assessments of character which can pass for biographical sketches, and which begin to be formed during the subjects' own careers, partly at the hands of critics and cartoonists. For example, the extracts in this chapter offer some material for questioning whether Gladstone was humourless or Disraeli was unprincipled.

The second purpose is to assess the significance of the interplay of personality with contemporary events. The periods when Disraeli and Gladstone exert the greatest influence on politics do not coincide. After the Corn Law crisis Disraeli's greatest impact is between 1866 and 1878, when the Conservative Party is very different from what it would have been without him. Although Gladstone was a prominent Liberal figure well before 1868, and Prime Minister for the next six years, the Liberal Party is not at this time very different from what it would have been without him. From 1878 to 1894, however, his re-entry into politics is of enormous significance for the way events turned out, especially in relation to Irish policy, radicalism and the unity of the Liberal Party.

Beyond the broad strokes of major biographies, historical writing has enhanced our understanding of the interplay of personality and major issues. Over the decades works have appeared by W.E. Williams on Gladstone's rise to Liberal leadership, Michael Baker on Gladstone and radicalism, Donald Southgate on Conservative leadership and E.J. Feuchtwanger on Disraeli and Conservative organisation, as well as books mentioned in other chapters. Diaries and correspondence, published and unpublished, are fertile sources of insight into personality, for the light they cast on the correspondents and also on third parties whom they discuss. They reinforce our impression that Disraeli never shed his tendency to view events and society with a novelist's eye, while Gladstone saw events in terms of his religious and moral duty.

Among Disraeli and Gladstone's contemporaries the person who has the greatest influence on politics is Queen Victoria, not only through her personal predisposition towards Disraeli and against Gladstone, but also for the general influence which her opinions have on the people, from the aristocracy, through the protagonists of 'high politics' to the great mass of middle- and working-class citizens. If we are to add just two more names of figures whose presence on the political stage is decisive during the ascendency of Disraeli and Gladstone, they would be Joseph Chamberlain and Charles Parnell.

The influence of these five complex characters, with all the contradictions of their origins, beliefs and careers, helps us to demolish not only the stereotypes of Gladstone and Disraeli, but also of the Victorian age itself.

1 Disraeli, Gladstone and Queen Victoria

(a) 'I cannot find him very agreeable'

[There are many published collections of extracts from Queen Victoria's letters and journals. A single source has been used here for ease of reference.]

JOURNAL 16 March 1852

5 [Mrs. Disraeli] is very vulgar, not so much in her appearance, as in her way of speaking; he is most singular, – thoroughly Jewish looking, a livid complexion, dark eyes and eyebrows and black ringlets. The expression is disagreeable, but I did not find him so to talk to. He has a very bland manner, and his language is very
10 flowery.

JOURNAL 19 March 1862

[Sir C. Phipps] showed me a very satisfactory paper from Mr. Gladstone [Chancellor of the Exchequer] on the subject [of allowances for the Queen's children]. Then saw Mr. Gladstone for
15 a little while, who was very kind and feeling. We talked of the state of the country. He spoke with such unbounded admiration and appreciation of my beloved Albert, saying no one could ever replace him.

MEMORANDUM 3 December 1868

20 I saw Mr. Gladstone at twenty minutes past five, he having come from Hawarden with General Grey. I said I knew he had consented to form a Government. He was most cordial and kind in his manner, and nothing could be more satisfactory than the whole interview.

25 TO THE CROWN PRINCESS OF PRUSSIA 25 September 1869
Mr. Gladstone left this morning. I cannot find him very agreeable, and he talks so very much. He looks dreadfully ill.

MEMORANDUM 25 June 1871
Mr. Gladstone spoke to me on the subject of Ireland this afternoon,
30 and on the wish expressed again and again that there should be a Royal residence there, and said that a motion on the subject was about to be brought in, to which an answer must be given. We went over the old ground, the pretensions of the Irish to have more done for them than the Welsh or English; the visits to Scotland
35 being in no one way political or connected with the wishes of the people, but merely because the climate and scenery are so healthy and beautiful, and the people so charming, so loyal, and the residence there of the greatest possible advantage (to mind and body) to our family, myself, and everyone connected with me and
40 my Household. That, therefore, to press and urge this was unreasonable. . .

TO THE CROWN PRINCESS OF PRUSSIA 17 February 1872
Our Government here does not get on very well. They have contrived to get so very unpopular. Mr. Gladstone is a very
45 dangerous Minister – and so wonderfully unsympathetic. I have felt this very much, but find his own followers and colleagues complain fully as much.

MEMORANDUM 17 February 1874
I saw Mr. Gladstone at quarter to three to-day. I began by saying
50 what extraordinary things had occurred since I had seen him, and how very unexpected the result of the elections was . . . .

We then talked of the causes of the great defeat of the Government in the elections. . . . I could, of course, not tell him that it was greatly owing to his own unpopularity, and to the
55 want of confidence people had in him. . . . After agreeing to approve [the resignation honours] and discussing the individual claims, I asked him what I could do for him? to which he replied 'Oh! nothing.'

Queen Victoria in her Letters and Journals, ed. Christopher Hibbert, 1984, pp 90, 163, 208–9, 212, 227, 235–6

Questions

a What did Victoria appreciate in Gladstone in the years before 1869?

b In what ways did Wales, Scotland and Ireland bedevil relations between the Queen and Gladstone in this period?

★ *c* From the evidence of your wider reading, what were Gladstone's motives for refusing a title in 1874 (and 1885 – see extract *e*)?

(b) *'Lay it on with a trowel'*

[To Matthew Arnold, in a conversation shortly before his death,
60 Disraeli said:] 'You have heard me called a flatterer, and it is true. Everyone likes flattery; and when you come to royalty, you should lay it on with a trowel'. . . .

HOUSE OF COMMONS, Friday, midnight [April 16, 1875] – Mr. Disraeli. . . returned home late last night, somewhat anxious
65 and wearied, when he found his room blazing, and perfumed, with the gems and jewels of Nature; and presenting in its appearance, and its associations, the most striking contrast to the scene he had just quitted.

He could not refrain from blessing the gracious tenderness that
70 had deigned to fill his lonely home with fragrance and beauty!

Such incidents outweigh all earthly honors; they sustain energy, sweeten toil, and soften many sorrows.

The Life of Benjamin Disraeli, G.E. Buckle, Vol. VI, 1920, pp 463–4

(c) *'Wisest of counsellors'*

JOURNAL 20 February 1874

I saw Mr. Disraeli at quarter to three to-day. He reported good
75 progress. . . . He knelt down and kissed hands, saying: 'I plight my troth to the kindness of Mistresses'!

JOURNAL 24 November 1875

Received a box from Mr. Disraeli, with the very important news that the Government has purchased the Viceroy of Egypt's share in
80 the Suez Canal for four millions, which gives us complete security for India, and altogether places us in a very safe position! An immense thing. It is entirely Mr. Disraeli's doing.

JOURNAL 14 March 1876

Heard, on getting up, that the second reading of the [Empress of
85 India] Titles Bill had been carried by 105! – an immense majority. It is to be hoped now no more stupid things will be said, and that the matter will be dropped. I cannot understand how the quite incorrect rumour can have got about, that I did not care for it; it is really too bad.

90 TO BEACONSFIELD 27 June 1877

The Queen must write to Lord Beaconsfield again and with the greatest earnestness on the very critical state of affairs. From so many does she hear of the great anxiety evinced that the Government should take a firm, bold line. This delay – this uncertainty, by
95 which, abroad, we are losing our prestige and our position, while Russia is advancing and will be before Constantinople in no time!

Then the Government will be fearfully blamed and the Queen so humiliated that she thinks she would abdicate at once. Be bold!

TO THE CROWN PRINCESS OF PRUSSIA 15 February 1878

100 Mr. Gladstone goes on like a madman. I never saw anything to equal the want of patriotism and the want of proper decency in Members of Parliament. It is a miserable thing to be a constitutional Queen and to be unable to do what is right. I would gladly throw all up and retire into quiet.

105 TO BEACONSFIELD 3 April 1880

This is a terrible telegram [announcing the defeat of the Conservatives]. The Queen cannot deny she. . .thinks it a great calamity for the country and the peace of Europe.

TO [HENRY] PONONBY 4 April 1880

110 The great alarm in the country is Mr. Gladstone, the Queen perceives and she will sooner abdicate than send for or have communication with that half-mad firebrand who will soon ruin everything and be a Dictator.

Others but herself may submit to his democratic rule, but not the 115 Queen.

She thinks he himself don't [*sic*] wish for or expect it.

TO THE CROWN PRINCESS OF PRUSSIA 14 September 1880

Mr. Gladstone is not what he was – he is *très baissé* [cast down] and really a little crazy. He has not recovered his illness yet and I doubt 120 (and fervently hope) he won't be able to go through another session.

JOURNAL 19 April 1881

Received the sad news that dear Lord Beaconsfield had passed away. I am most terribly shocked and grieved, for dear Lord 125 Beaconsfield was one of my best, most beloved, and kindest of friends, as well as wisest of counsellors. His loss is irreparable to me and the country. To lose such a pillar of strength, at such a moment, is dreadful!

Queen Victoria in her Letters and Journals, ed. Christopher Hibbert, 1984, pp 236, 241–2, 245, 250, 260, 264, 268

Questions

a Use extract *b* to qualify Disraeli's own comment that he flattered the Queen. Was their relationship founded on flattery, or did Disraeli's blandishments merely smooth their path?

★ *b* What did Victoria and Disraeli each give to the other in their friendship?

c Do the 1877 and 1878 entries (lines 90 to 104) suggest differences between Victoria and Disraeli in their attitudes to imperialism and foreign policy?

★ *d* Was Victoria correct in considering herself powerless as a constitutional monarch? What influence did she attempt to bring to bear after the 1880 election?

e What is the significance of the phrase, 'at such a moment' (line 127)?

(d) 'Enough to kill any man'

Hawarden Jan. 5 1883

130 . . . . After breakfast Mr. Gladstone put on a little Inverness cape and a straw hat, and invited me to walk round and round the square garden. Talked much of his health, excellent except in one point, that the night's sleep, eight hours or so, which is what keeps his brain and nervous energy going, he cannot depend on. Much 135 discourse on this. He generally had neuralgia at the end of a session, and pays for his work in that way. He spoke of his troubles. 'The Queen alone', he said fiercely, 'is enough to kill any man'. . . .

The Marquess of Crewe, [*Biography of*] *Lord Rosebery*, Vol. I, 1931, pp 164–5

(e) 'A good deal of harm'

TO GLADSTONE 7 August 1881

The Queen has to thank Mr. Gladstone for his regular and 140 interesting reports of the proceedings in the House of Commons, many of which are of a most disgraceful character. But how can you expect better from so many Members of such low and revolutionary views who are now in the House of Commons?

TO THE PRINCE OF WALES 27 May 1882

145 The state of affairs – this dreadfully Radical Government which contains many thinly-veiled Republicans – and the way in which they have truckled to the Home Rulers – as well as the utter disregard of all my opinions which after 45 years of experience ought to be considered, all make me very miserable . . . .

150 JOURNAL 25 June 1882

I told [Lord Hartington] I wished he were at the head of the Government, instead of Mr. Gladstone. He admitted that Mr. Gladstone had a leaning towards the Irish, as he is always excusing them to me!

155 TO THE CROWN PRINCESS OF PRUSSIA 2 October 1883

Mr. Gladstone's journey well deserves blame [he had made a sea

journey to Scandinavia on impulse]. But can you imagine that he is so ignorant of what is going on that he never knew till the pilot told him when they were on the way to Copenhagen that the Emperor
160 of Russia was there? He trusts Russia, hates Austria and don't like Germany [*sic*]. Republican France and Italy are all he cares for.

TO GLADSTONE 30 October 1883

The Queen has been much distressed by all she heard and read lately of the deplorable condition of the Homes of the Poor in our
165 great towns . . . . She cannot but think that there are questions of less importance than this, which are under discussion, and might wait till one involving the very existence of thousands – nay millions – had been fully considered by the Government.

JOURNAL 5 February 1885

170 Dreadful news after breakfast. Khartoum fallen, Gordon's fate uncertain! All greatly distressed. Sent for Sir H. Ponsonby, who was horrified. It is too fearful. The Government is alone to blame, by refusing to send the expedition till it was too late. Telegraphed *en clair* [openly] to Mr. Gladstone, Lord Granville, and Lord
175 Hartington, expressing how dreadfully shocked I was at the news, all the more so when one felt it might have been prevented.

TO GLADSTONE 13 June 1885

Mr. Gladstone mentioned in his last letter but one, his intention of proposing some [resignation] honours. But before she considers
180 these, she wishes to offer him an Earldom, as a mark of her recognition of his long and distinguished services . . . .

TO [GEORGE] GOSCHEN 31 January 1886

Mr. Gladstone really intends to bring forward Home Rule, and I trust that the line you and Lord Hartington and other influential
185 people will take will soon bring a good many Liberals to their senses and open their eyes.

JOURNAL 30 July 1886

After luncheon saw Mr. Gladstone, who looked pale and nervous . . . . Spoke of education, it being carried too far, and he entirely
190 agreed that it ruined the health of the higher classes uselessly, and rendered the working classes unfitted for good servants and labourers. I then wished him good-bye, shaking hands with him, and he kissed mine.
[In 1892 Gladstone took office again, raising what Victoria thought
195 of as the spectre of Home Rule. He retired finally in 1894].

JOURNAL 19 May 1898

Heard at breakfast time that poor Mr. Gladstone, who has been

hopelessly ill for some time and had suffered severely, had passed away quite peacefully this morning at five. He was very clever and
200 full of ideas for the bettering and advancement of the country, always most loyal to me personally, and ready to do anything for the Royal Family, but alas! I am sure involuntarily, he did at times a good deal of harm. He had a wonderful power of speaking and carrying the masses with him.

Queen Victoria in her Letters and Journals, ed. Christopher Hibbert, 1984, pp 270, 274, 275, 283, 289, 296, 299, 337

Questions

a From the evidence of these extracts who was more responsible for bad communication between Gladstone and the Queen?

b What new factors in the relationship appear in this period?

★ *c* What part did Victoria play in the political developments of 1885–6? Was her influence strictly constitutional?

d Do these extracts suggest the limitations of Gladstone's radicalism?

2 Disraeli dissected

(a) Mary Anne's balance sheet

[Mrs. Mary Anne Disraeli's list of her husband's characteristics and her own]

	[His]	[Hers]
	Very calm	Very effervescent
	Manners grave and almost sad	Gay and happy-looking when speaking
5	Never irritable	Very irritable
	Bad humoured	Good humoured
	Warm in love, but cold in friendship.	Cold in love, but warm in friendship
10	Very patient	No patience
	Very studious	Very idle
	Very generous	Only generous to those she loves
15	Often says what he does not think	Never says anything she does not think.
	It is impossible to find out who he likes or dislikes from his manner. He does not show his feelings.	Her manner is quite different and to those she likes she shows her feelings.
20	No vanity	Much vanity
	Conceited	No conceit

No self-love	Much self-love
He is seldom amused	Everything amuses her
He is a genius	She is a dunce
25 He is to be depended on to a certain degree.	She is not to be depended on
His whole soul is devoted to politics and ambition.	She has no ambition and hates politics.

D.H. Elletson, *Maryannery*, 1959, pp 149–50

(b) The Political Novelist

. . . I admit that if any man be entirely destitute of all claim to
30 indulgence, it is the subject of this biography. Personality is his mighty weapon, which he has used like a gladiator whose only object is at all events to inflict a deadly wound upon his adversary, and not like a chivalrous knight, who will at any risk obey the laws of the tournament . . . .

35 Who can answer a political novel? Libels the most scandalous may be insinuated, the best and wisest men may be represented as odious, the purest intentions and most devoted patriotism may be maligned under the outline of a fictitious character. The personal satirist is truly the pest of society, and any method might be
40 considered justifiable by which he could be hunted down . . . .

We are naturally inclined, as it has been often said, to imitate what we admire. If such exhibitions in the house of Commons continue for the next twenty years, and such criticisms be penned, in which all mention of right and wrong is as quietly omitted as in
45 the political writings of Machiavelli, not only will the style of parliamentary debating be changed, but our politicians will degenerate, until there be no trace in them of that genuine English manly morality which has so highly distinguished the nation . . . .

Thomas Macknight, *The Right Honourable Benjamin Disraeli, M.P., A Literary and Political Biography Addressed to the New Generation*, 1854, pp 7, 9

(c) Cautious compliments

I have I think seen more of Disraeli and got a juster appreciation of
50 him than ever before. There is no doubt as to his genius – and his breadth of view. He detests details and always looks to the principle or rather the *idea* of any question. He is in fact unable to deal with details. He does no work. For many days past he has not put pen to paper.
55 M [ontagu] Corry [Disraeli's secretary] is in fact Prime Minister and on the whole does not manage amiss or abuse much his power.

He is in private life amiable.

Sir Arthur Hardinge, *The Life of Henry Howard Molyneux Herbert, Fourth Earl of Carnarvon, 1831–1890*, Vol. II, 1925, p 78

Questions

a What are the uses of personal accounts by the family, friends and critics of a political figure? What pitfalls must historians avoid in the use of such material?

b Comment on the proposition that if Disraeli's loving wife criticises him, the criticism must be valid.

c Were Disraeli's criticisms of contemporaries more or less effective in the literary form than they would have been if openly expressed?

d What qualities of a statesman does Lord Carnarvon identify? Why does Carnarvon express reservations about Disraeli? There are clues also in Chapter III, section 5(*a*), and section 6(*d*).

3 Glimpses of Gladstone

(a) Gladstone's dialectic

March 2 [1870]
I went at [Granville's] suggestion to see Gladstone whom I found at
Carlton Terrace in the afternoon. I shall not easily forget my
interview with him. He argued passionately against all coercive
measures, especially against giving power to the Irish Government
5 to suspend the Habeas Corpus Act in disturbed districts. Bright he
said would certainly resign sooner than agree to such a power . . . .

I made the best fight I could, but it is impossible to get the best of
Gladstone in argument. His ingenuity in shifting his ground, and in
probing every weak point in his adversary's armour render him
10 almost invincible. Unfortunately he is often led astray by his own
subtilty, and thus gives exaggerated weight in council to arguments
useful perhaps in debate but more plausible than sound. I have
heard that Palmerston one day when he had been sorely tried by
Gladstone's dialectics said to a friend, 'You remember the anecdote
15 about Pitt when he was asked what was the [first] quality of a
statesman? He answered, "patience", and the second? patience –
and the third? – patience. But Pitt did not know Gladstone!'

Camden 3rd Series Vol. 90 (Camden Miscellary Vol. 21), *A Journal of Events during the Gladstone Ministry 1868–1874 (1st Earl of Kimberley's Journal)*, 1958, p 12

(b) *Tribute to the whole man*

The combination of popular sympathies with traditional inspiration, of courageous faith in the future with profound veneration of 20 the past, forms an admirable foundation for the character of an English statesman; but it is not very frequently found in anything like an equally balanced perfection. The ambition which spurs a man in the race of public life too often mars the sincerity of devotion to principle. Magnificent powers of debate are not often 25 accompanied with minute mastery of details in administration. The subtlety which traces a question through all possible issues is not usually conjoined with the sweep of thought that commands confusion into order. Susceptibility to the charm of venerable religious forms is rarely associated with the courage that holds to 30 practical justice as the truest faith. Swift facility and patient drudgery are not generally possible to the same mind. The statesman and the leader of the people are for the most part different men. But, standing on Blackheath on that October day [in 1878] when Mr. Gladstone addressed, not his own constituents 35 only, but the people of England, we received an impression of transcendental personal power, and almost prophetic inspiration, for a great mission such as is never made by a merely oratorical display. The strong resonant voice and honest intonation, the unrivalled facility of expression, all were striking in their way. But 40 all were nothing compared with the unspoken, because unspeakable, depth of sympathy which was the real spell that held them fast.

British Quarterly, quoted in *The Political Life of the Right Hon. W.E. Gladstone,* Illustrated from *Punch,* Vol. I, 1898, p 311

(c) *Gladstone's humour and its limits*

Early in 1883 I first became aquainted with Mr. Gladstone in the ever hospitable house of Mr. F. Leverson Gower at Holmbury 45 . . . . The Prime Minister was in great spirits, and talked on every kind of subject, from the rapacity of publishers, to the Channel Tunnel, which he said he would never oppose . . . .

The first evening [of a subsequent house party] Mr. Gladstone was in a humorous vein. He had been playing a rubber with Lord 50 Granville and his host, in the midst of which I heard him descanting on the origin and nature of Protestantism. A propos of which he told how one day a certain Damascus Jew presented himself at the British Consulate and asked for British protection on the ground that he was a Protestant. How so, they asked, why do you call 55 yourself a Protestant? 'I eat pork', was the answer, 'and I don't believe in God.'

Later in the day Disraeli had . . . come under discussion and Sir

George Dasent had been describing the flow of eloquence that had poured from his lips at a Royal Academy banquet, where he
60 enlarged upon the inspiration which it was to him to come year by year and feast his eyes upon these triumphs of British Art. When they were walking around the rooms afterwards, Dasent felt a hand upon his shoulder, and heard the voice of Dizzy whispering in his ear: 'Did you ever see such a collection of rubbish in your life?' 'Did
65 he say that?' exclaimed Mr. Gladstone. 'Oh dear! oh dear! oh dear!' 'Yes', replied Sir George, 'rather funny, wasn't it?' 'Funny! you call it', the old man thundered indignantly; 'I call it devilish'.

Sir James Rennell Rodd, *Social and Diplomatic Memories 1884–1893*, 1922, pp 36, 38–9

Questions

a Use extracts *a* and *b* to show how character traits can be given a pejorative and a favourable gloss by critics and enthusiasts.

b What characteristics of Gladstone's religious beliefs are revealed by extracts *b* and *c*?

c According to extract *c*, what was it about Disraeli that disgusted Gladstone?

VIII Recessional

This chapter is so called in relation to the theme of this book, and it begins and ends with the deaths of the Earl of Beaconsfield and Gladstone. For our understanding of people's motives and opinions it is fortunate that the Victorians were not addicted to the principle '*de mortuis nil nisi bonum*' (speak only good of the dead), for among the eulogies we find also reflective critical comments.

There is a sympathetic and an unsympathetic view of Gladstone's second ministry. Was it 'unlucky' – even, perhaps, suffering the aftermath of Disraeli's foreign policy and his neglect of Irish affairs? Or did Gladstone reap the whirlwind that he himself had sown from 1878 to 1880, in that he conjured up expectations in Ireland, raised the temperature of debate in the Commons and set a high moral standard in foreign policy? In office his party's programme and political will were not equal to the events that unfolded.

As to the period after 1886, historiography has concentrated on the problems of the Liberals. They are represented as indecisive in policy, beset by the defection of the Liberal Unionists (examined in recent scholarship by M.C. Hurst), weakened by the rival attraction of populist Imperialism on the one hand and socialism on the other.

Yet the Conservatives did not have the period 1886 to 1895 all their own way either. Their dependence on the Liberal Unionists for a majority influenced their programme, as the Liberals' dependence on the Irish Nationalists did theirs. Neither party had a policy with strong rationale. Balfour's 'policy of thorough' in Ireland, mitigated by land reform and the development of light railways, brought some temporary quiet there, while the major domestic reform of the period, the development of local government, can hardly be claimed as a partisan Conservative achievement.

In a sense, as in the 1846–66 period, events overseas and social and economic change at home took the initiative from the parties in parliament. The classic gladiatorial battle between Gladstone and Disraeli, with their distinctive brands of Liberalism and Conservatism, was over.

1 The passing of Lord Beaconsfield

(a) Gladstone's public tribute

[Gladstone moves for the erection of a monument.]

The career of Lord Beaconsfield is, in many respects, the most remarkable one in parliamentary history. For my own part, I know but one that can fairly be compared to it in regard to the emotion of surprise, and when viewed as a whole an emotion, I might say, of
5 wonder, and that is the career, and especially the earlier career, of Mr. Pitt. Lord Beaconsfield's name is associated with great Constitutional changes, at least with one great Constitutional change, in regard to which I think it will ever be admitted, at least I never can scruple to admit, that its arrival was accelerated by his
10 personal act (hear, hear). I will not dwell upon that, but I will simply mention the close association of his name with that important change in the principle of the Parliamentary franchise. It is also associated with great European transactions, and great European arrangements . . . .

15 There were certain great qualities of the deceased statesman on which I think it right to touch. His extraordinary intellectual powers are as well understood by others as by me, and they are not proper subjects for our present commendation. But there were other great qualities – qualities not merely intellectual in the sense
20 of being dissociated from conduct, but qualities immediately connected with conduct . . . .

I speak, for example, of such as these – his strength of will; his long-sighted persistency of purpose, reaching from the first entrance on the avenue of life to its very close; his remarkable
25 powers of self-government; and last, but not least, of all, his great Parliamentary courage, a quality in which I, who have been associated in the course of my life with scores of Ministers, have never known but two whom I could pronounce to be his equal. There were some other points in his character upon which I cannot
30 refrain from saying one word. I wish to express the admiration I have always felt for his strong sympathy with his race, for the sake of which he was always ready to risk popularity and influence. A like sentiment I feel towards the strength of his sympathy with that brotherhood to which he thought, and justly thought, he was
35 entitled to belong – the brotherhood of men of letters . . . .

I wish to record in this place and at this hour my firm conviction that in all the judgements ever delivered by the late Lord Beaconsfield on myself, he was never actuated by sentiments of personal antipathy (cheers).

The 'Standard', 10 May 1881, pp 75–78 in *Gladstone Speeches and Pamphlets*, Vol. XXVII, St Deiniol's Library, Hawarden, M 34–9 G2

(b) *The Gladstones' private musings*

40 LONDON Fri. April 22 to Fri. 29 [1881] – . . . To think of my never mentioning Lord Beaconsfield's death on April 19 and all the consequent rush of highest flown praise. First-rate nonsense rampaged for a week. Papa telegraphed to offer a public funeral, but this was refused. Dr. Liddon's allusion was full of dignity and 45 justice and there was something very awful in his concluding words: only in so far as they are like God, will they be acceptable to God, or some such words. He quoted a German pessimist poet who said that 'sadness and aspiration' were chief ingredients of genuine universal poetry. The sermon was on the perplexities of 50 life . . . .

LONDON, Mon. May 2 – . . . Father said Lord Beaconsfield had lowered the whole standard of morality in politics, specially among Conservatives, in a lesser degree among Liberals. I asked why then he proposed a national memorial of him? 'Parliament and the 55 nation had backed him up, they were responsible for him, a statue shd. be given to a man according to the place he occupied in the public estimation. History must eventually judge as to the result. If all the wits in the world were gathered into one man, and that man occupied the whole of his lifetime in the judgement of a moral 60 action, he would be incompetent to do it.'

Mary Gladstone, *Her Diaries and Letters*, ed. Lucy Masterman, 1930, pp 224–5

Questions

a Identify the change in the franchise and the 'great European transactions' referred to in extract *a*, lines 12–14.

b How does Gladstone's estimation of Beaconsfield vary in public and private? Can you account for the difference?

c Gladstone professed to have no personal animosity towards Disraeli. Do these extracts support this proposition?

2 Phoenix Park

(a) *O'Shea mediates between Gladstone and Parnell*

1 Albert Mansions
S.W. [London]
April 13 1882

[O'Shea has corresponded with Gladstone about Parnell's conditions for discouraging agrarian protest.]

My dear Sir,

5 At the risk of appearing importunate, I reply to your letter of the 11th.

I did not mean to convey to you that the plan which I proposed to you in June could be adapted to present circumstances, but I assert that if you had agreed to it, there would have been no Land League Convention, the Court would not have been blocked, the
10 gaols would have been empty. A reasonable and unacrimonious argument for the revision of certain clauses relating to Arrears, Improvements and Purchase, would have had the place of the present brutalities of debate, and the burthen on the Exchequer would have been light indeed, compared with the immediate gain
15 to the Empire in peace, order and good will . . . .

[O'Shea gives his credentials at length as a spokesman for Parnell.] By the use of this influence I brought Mr. Parnell within the sphere of moderate counsels in June. On Tuesday he observed that the government must regret having refused my offer. Your
20 letter of the 11th proves this to have been a mistake on his part.

However, I will try to mediate again. This time of course Mr. Parnell has no part in the initiative.

The primary questions are these. Have the Government yet discovered that Mr. Parnell is a personage exercising immense
25 power in Ireland and considerable influence in England? Do they believe that the forces behind him would mutiny if he were to commend them moderation? If the answer to the first be Yes, and to the second No, it is evident that you would do well to listen to me, because what I was able to do before, I might be able to do
30 again [O'Shea develops in further detail his suggestions for Irish land and administrative reform] . . . .

I have written freely, I hope you will not consider too freely. I regret the length of my letter and I remain,

Yours very faithfully,

W.H. O'Shea

British Library, Add. MS. 44269, folios 18, 20, 21, 25

(b) Cavendish goes to Dublin

House of Commons

[To Gladstone] 4th [May 1882]

My dear Sir,

I need scarecely say that I am very grateful for the kindness with
35 which you spoke to me this evening.

I am anxious, and I think with a fair view to usefulness, to make the better aquaintance of Lord Frederick Cavendish.

I repeat that I feel most deeply the sense of my responsibility, but I have great hope.

40 I remain

Yours very truly

W.H. O'Shea

British Library, Add. MS. 44269, folio 34

(c) Assassination

LONDON, Sat. May 6 1882 . . . . There were unwonted lights in the windows, and seeing a number of people up and Smith stammering 'bad news' at 1st I thought it was Papa. Then they said Ireland and Lord Frederick, and I rushed to Eddy [Hamilton] and
40 learnt the too terrible truth. He was stabbed and killed about ½ past 7 in Phoenix Park close to the Viceregal Lodge. Mr. Burke with whom he was walking also killed . . . .

Mary Gladstone, *Her diaries and letters*, ed. Lucy Masterman, 1930, p 249

(d) Nationalists repudiate the crime

1 Albert Mansions
S.W. [London]
May 6 1882

[To Gladstone]

My dear Sir,

I am so busy about another part of the business that I have not yet been able to make out the list of suspects, but I hope to do so before
45 post hour.

Mr. Parnell has called a meeting of his friends for 2 o'clock on Monday at which it will be decided to give the Government their unanimous support in the division on Sir M. Hicks Beach's motion. There are a few grumblings but they will be immediately stifled.

Yours very truly
W.H. O'Shea

May 7 1882

Dear Mr. Gladstone

50 Davitt was anxious to go to Dublin but has been dissuaded.

He has drafted the Manifesto, as it was thought best to allow him to do so. It is in somewhat high-flown language; it denounces in the strongest terms the assassinations at a time that there was a prospect of better things for Ireland, and the murder of a friendly stranger
55 coming to Ireland for the first time. It calls upon the people to use their strongest efforts to bring the murderers to justice, and it is signed by Messrs. Parnell, Dillon and Davitt.

Yours most faithfully,
W.H. O'Shea

British Library, Add. MS. 44269, folios 37–9

Questions

a What measure of the British Government in Ireland had Parnell been agitating to have withdrawn?

★ *b* Does the evidence of your wider reading support O'Shea's assertion that agrarian disturbances would abate if the measure referred to in question *a* were withdrawn?

c Why had it been necessary for Parnell to communicate with Gladstone through O'Shea?

d What alteration did the Phoenix Park murders bring about in Parnell's stance?

3 Gordon

(a) Gordon awaits help

December 13 [1884]

. . . I send this journal, for I have little hopes of saving it if the town falls . . . . Even if the town falls under the nose of the Expeditionary Force, it will not, in my opinion, justify the abandonment of Senaar and Kassala, or of the Equatorial Province, 5 by Her Majesty's Government. All that is absolutely necessary is, for fifty of the Expeditionary Force to get on board a steamer and come up to Halfeyeh, and thus let their presence be felt; this is not asking much, but it must happen *at once*; or it will (as usual) be too late. A soldier deserted to the Arabs today from the North Fort. 10 The buglers on the roof, being short of stature, are put on boxes to enable them to fire over the parapet; one with the recoil of rifle was knocked right over, and caused considerable excitement. We thought he was killed, by the noise he made in his fall. The Arabs fired their Krupps continually into towns from the South front, but 15 no one takes any notice of it. The Arabs at Goba only fired one shell at the Palace to-day, which burst in the air.

December 14th – Arabs fired two shells at the Palace this morning; 546 ardebs dhoora! in store; also 83,525 okes of biscuit! [1 ardeb = 5½ bushels: dhoora = Indian millet: 1 oke = $2\frac{4}{5}$ lb] 10.30 A.M. 20 The steamers are down at Omdurman, engaging the Arabs, consequently I am on tenterhooks! 11.30 A.M. steamers returned; The Bordeen was struck by a shell in her battery; we had only one man wounded. We are going to send down the Bordeen tomorrow with this journal. If I was in command of the two hundred men of 25 the Expeditionary Force, which are all that are necessary for the movement, I should stop just below Halfeyeh, and attack the Arabs at that place before I came on here to Khartoum. I should then communicate with the North Fort, and act according to circumstances.

30 NOW MARK THIS, if the Expeditionary Force, and I ask for no more than two hundred men, does not come in ten days, *the town*

may fall; and I have done my best for the honour of our country. Good bye

C.G. GORDON

You send me no information, though you have lots of money.

C.G.G.

[Gordon was killed, and Khartoum taken, on 26th January 1885]

The Journals of Major-General C.G. Gordon, C.B., At Khartoum, 1885, pp 394–5

(b) Gordon beyond help

The external troubles with which the Government was surrounded
35 darkened and deepened during 1884 and 1885. One great trouble was that in Egypt [i.e. Sudan], where the Mahdi still held his own, and where the hero Gordon was still shut up in Khartoum. There was a strange, and to this day an unaccountable, delay about the measures to be taken for Gordon's rescue. People said that the
40 Government had no hope of being able to do anything to save him; and a Government is in sore straits when people believe that there is something that it ought to do and cannot even try to do . . . . Perhaps the Government had only too good reason to believe that Gordon was beyond the help of any relief expedition. The trial
45 had to be made, however, and the expedition was put under the command of a man as competent as could be found in England . . . .

No commander could have forced his way under such difficulties to Khartoum in time to rescue General Gordon . . . . It would be needless to say that the death of Gordon was a terrible blow to the
50 Liberal Government. Gordon was an ideal hero; and an Administration of saints and sages could not have been saved from reproach if an expedition for such a purpose had failed under its management, although by no fault of those who sent it out or those who conducted it.

Justin MacCarthy, *A History of Our Own Times from 1880 to the Diamond Jubilee,* 1897, pp 159–61

Questions

- ★ *a* By what stages had the British become involved in the Sudan?
- *b* Identify the commander referred to in extract *b*, line 46.
- ★ *c* By comparing extracts *a* and *b*, and relating them to your wider studies, comment on McCarthy's assertion that Gordon could not have been rescued.
- *d* What political damage did Gordon's death cause to Gladstone's government?

4 The Third Reform Act

The Government, although evidently weakened and sinking, did not

go out of office without having done some good and substantial work for the constitution and for the country . . . . There were two distinct problems to be dealt with: first, the question of franchise, and next,
5 the question of redistribution of seats . . . . With regard to the distribution of seats, the most flagrant anomalies and injustice were still existing. In some cases pitiful little boroughs with only a few hundred inhabitants returned as many representatives as some great and important counties . . . .
10 Mr. Gladstone . . . divided his great reform scheme into two separate portions; that is to say, into two separate bills. The first was the Franchise Bill, which he introduced into the House of Commons on February 29th 1884. The bill, he said, was introduced in fulfilment of a pledge, in obedience to a widely expressed demand, and for the
15 purpose of adding strength to the State. He declined to argue the case of the classes to be enfranchised, as that case had been admitted in regard to borough populations fifteen [should be seventeen] years before, and had been completely approved by the experience of those fifteen [seventeen] years . . . . 'I take my stand upon the
20 broad principle that the enfranchisement of capable citizens, be they fewer be they many – and if they be many, so much the better – is an addition to the strength of the State.'

Justin McCarthy, *A History of Our Own Times from 1880 to the Diamond Jubilee*, 1897, pp 165–7

Questions

★ *a* Which people were enfranchised in 1884? How far short of universal suffrage did this fall?

b Why did Gladstone not feel it necessary to argue in principle for an extension of the franchise?

★ *c* What electoral implications within the Liberal party did the 1885 redistribution of seats have?

5 A maze of events: 1885–6

(a) Tory and Liberal remedies for Ireland

[A speech by Lord Rosebery at Paisley, Autumn 1885, criticising Conservative policy.]

. . . . There were frequent outrages in Ireland. But this is the moment at which the Tories decided, with a light heart, not to renew any part of the Crimes Act . . . . Day by day, year by year, in season and out of season, in bed and out of bed, Lord Carnarvon is engaged in pouring little drops of oil – infinitesimal drops of oil on
5 the stormy waters of Irish wrath and Irish discontent. When the cruet-stand fails he falls back on the Consolidated Fund, and if the British tax payer does not weary in well-doing neither will he. What is the result? The Irish vote is to be cast against the Liberal
10 Party . . . .

[Rosebery then introduces Liberal policy:] What is proposed is this, as I understand, that Ireland should be treated as a colony [note that no word then existed for the more equal relationship which later existed between Britain and the Dominions], and that the
15 Crown should be the only link between Ireland and the mother-country.

. . . . Is Ireland loyal to the British connection, or is she not? If I had the power, and if I were convinced that Ireland were loyal to the connection with this country, there would be no limits to the
20 concessions that I would offer to Ireland . . . .'

The Marquess of Crewe, *[Biography of] Lord Rosebery*, Vol. I, 1931, p 229

(b) Parnell calls the tune

Hawarden Castle
Chester

Dear Mrs. O'Shea, Dec. 19 [18]85

. . . . Up to this moment the Nationalists are the ostensible allies of the Government and opponents of the Liberals. By their means, the Government have gained and we have lost a majority in the towns. Under these circumstances, as there is irritation to soothe,
25 as well as prejudice to overcome, most of all there is novelty and strangeness to convert into familiar observation and reflection.

I think duty to the Government (as and while such), duty to my own party, and duty to the purpose in view, combine to require that I should hold my ground; should cherish the hope that the
30 Government will act; and that Mr. Parnell as the organ of what is now undeniably the Irish party should learn from them whether they will bring in a measure or proposition to deal with and settle the whole question of the future of Ireland . . . .

W.E. Gladstone

North Park
Eltham, Kent

Dear Mr. Gladstone, Dec. 23rd, 1885

I waited until today in the hope of hearing from you again before
35 replying to your letter of the 19th instant as I am anxious not to give you the trouble of reading any unnecessary letters, but I wished to tell you that I know the Alliance (I use your designation of it) between the Nationalists and the present Government has been faithfully carried out on both sides. Both have done all that
40 was expected of them. The Conservatives wanted the Irish vote, for which they were willing to undertake to do away with Coercion and they have both carried out their promises – but the Alliance goes no further. I know that Mr. Parnell never at any time expected them to attempt any scheme of the kind that I sent to you
45 for he has never at any time wavered from the belief, that he has

always felt, that you alone could carry it – and even at the eleventh hour he asked me on the eve of that division which brought in the present Government if I thought it possible to ascertain if you would consider a scheme for the settlement of the Irish question as
50 in that case if any hope could have been held out by you, the Irish vote would not have been given to the Conservatives . . . .

Mr. Parnell is anxious, I think, to understand your views fully before any vote of confidence comes on that he may know how to direct his party to act but I gather from your letter today there is a
55 possibilty of the Tories remaining in office for the present . . . .

Believe me,
Yours truly,
Katie O'Shea

British Library, Add. MS. 44269, folios 256–7, 261–2, 264

Questions

- ★ *a* In what circumstances did the Conservatives take office in 1885? How had the Irish Nationalists influenced the election result in the English towns? (extract *b*, line 23).
- *b* On what grounds does Rosebery advocate Liberal policy and criticise Conservative measures?
- *c* What light does extract *b* shed on the confusion existing in 1885–6?
- ★ *d* Why was Mrs O'Shea an intermediary between Parnell and Gladstone at this time? What was the potential for embarrassment to Gladstone from this situation?

6 Liberal Unionism is Born

(a) The Radical wing

[The first speech of the Unauthorised Programme] Warrington, September 8, 1885.

What is the Radical programme?. . .

We propose nothing extreme, I was going to say nothing new. We propose to extend the functions and powers of the local authorities. . . . . We propose to give the popular representative authorities
5 the right to obtain land for all public purposes at its fair value. . . . We propose also that the local authority in every district, under proper conditions, shall have power to let land for labourers' allotments, for artisans' dwellings, and for small holdings. . . .

There is another and a very important question on which I
10 should like to say a few words, and that is the freedom of the schools . . . . You might free the schools to-morrow without in the slightest degree affecting the position of the denominational system

. . . . At the present time the total of fees receivable in all the schools of England and Wales amount to a little over a million and a half,
15 and I believe an addition to the income tax of three farthings in the pound [0.3125 per cent], as one method of providing the money, would be sufficient to throw open to-morrow every schoolhouse in the land . . . .

There is a question of the revision of taxation. I think that
20 taxation ought to involve equality of sacrifice, and I do not see how this result is to be obtained except by some form of graduated taxation . . . .

What is Mr. Parnell's programme? He says that in his opinion the time has come to abandon altogether all attempts to obtain further
25 remedial measures or subsidiary reforms and to concentrate the efforts of the Irish representatives upon the securing of a single chamber, whose first object it will be to put a protective duty against all English manufactures. Then he says in the second place that he expects Whig and Tory will vie with one another in helping
30 him to a settlement on his own terms, and he says in the last place that if any party seeks to make that object impossible, he and his friends will make all things impossible for them . . . . This new programme of Mr. Parnell's involves a great extension of anything that we have hitherto understood by 'Home Rule' . . . . If this
35 claim were conceded, we might as well for ever abandon all hope of maintaining a United Kingdom.

Mr. [Joseph] Chamberlain's Speeches, ed. Charles W. Boyd, Vol. I, 1914, pp 189–91, 193, 241–2

(b) The 'moderate' wing

Goschen to Lord Hartington December 7 1885

I agree with your remark that 'the mess is the most inextricable into which a country ever got itself'; and I confess I see no satisfactory end, even if one had to choose a policy for oneself. I see
40 little difference in your views and mine as to the nearest future.

1. I do not think a coalition possible. You say you fancy overtures will be made to Parnell in the first instance? . . .

2. I agree with you that it may possibly be right to promise the Government independent support, if they reject the Parnell
45 alliance, and if, as I expect, Gladstone will be ready to grant what you and I would never agree to . . . . He will then find it difficult to form a Cabinet, or if he forms one, it will be a Radical Cabinet. Will Parnell support him? Even if he does, it may be possible for the moderate men to prevent his carrying out a crude design. But
50 don't let us allow things to come to that pass.

Hon. Arthur D. Elliott, *The Life of George Joachim Goschen,* Vol. I, 1911, p 318

Questions

a What was it that 'you and I would never agree to' (extract *b*, line 46)?

b In what specific details of extract *a* is Chamberlain conciliatory towards non-radical opinion? How might this have helped the various shades of unionist opinion to coalesce?

c By what catch-phrase did the land proposals of the Unauthorised Programme come to be identified?

d By comparing extracts *a* and *b*, assess whether Liberal Unionism was essentially positive or negative: that is, whether unionists were chiefly attracted to a programme or united in opposition to Gladstone.

★ *e* What were the main electoral implications of the secession of the Liberal Unionists in 1886?

7 Ireland again

Belfast, April 1st 1893

Ulster will fight, and fight to the death. The people have taken a resolution – deep, stern and irrevocable. Outwardly they do not seem so troubled as the Dubliners. They are quiet in their movements, moderate in their speech. They show no kind of alarm, for they know their own strength, and are fully prepared for the worst . . . .

They hold that Home Rule is at the bottom a religious movement, that by circuitous methods, and subterranean strategy, the religious reconquest of the island is sought; that the ignorant peasantry, composing the large majority of the electorate, are entirely in the hands of the priests, and that these black swarms of Papists have a congenital hatred of England, which must bring about separation. These are the opinions of thousands of eminent men whose ability is beyond argument, who have lived all their lives on the spot, who from childhood have had innumerable facilities for knowing the truth, whose interests are bound up with the prosperity of Ireland, and who, on every ground, are admittedly the best judges. Said Mr. Albert Quill, the Dublin barrister:–

'Mr. Gladstone, who in eighty-four years has spent a week in Ireland, puts aside Sir Edward Harland, who has built a fleet of great ships in an Irish port [Belfast], and sneers at the opinion of the Belfast deputation who have lived all their lives in Ireland . . . . '

But what are the Belfast men doing? *Imprimis* [first] they are working in what may be called the regular English methods, Unionist clubs are springing up in all directions . . . . The Ulster Anti-Repeal and Loyalist Association will during the month of

April hold over three hundred meetings in England, all manned by competent speakers. The Irish Unionist Association and the
30 Conservative Association are likewise doing excellent work, which is patent to everybody. But other associations which do not need public offices are flourishing like green bay trees, and their work is eminently suggestive. By virtue of an all-powerful introduction, I yesterday visited what may be called the Ulster war department,
35 and there saw regular preparation for an open campaign . . . . The tables are covered with documents connected with the sale and purchase of rifles and munitions of war . . ..

Ireland as it is and as it would be under Home Rule, by the Special Commissioner of the *Birmingham Daily Gazette*, 1893, pp 13–15

Questions

★ *a* What political developments gave rise to these manifestations of unionism in Ireland?
b What is the political significance of the source of this extract?
c In what ways does the writer of this article reveal his bias? What counterbalancing evidence of opinion in Ireland in 1893 would help us to have a more complete picture?

8 The passing of Gladstone

26 May 1898

I went to see Mr. Gladstone lying in state, several times. I stood in the reserved space and watched the crowd go surging past at the rate of 150 and at times 200 every minute. An orderly, well-dressed respectful crowd; patient and submissive to the police who allowed
5 no delay for expressing their sentiment and regrets. Scores of people passed by – hundreds I should say, without looking at the catafalque at all . . . .

This was so strange that many members of parliament standing by tried to analyse the feelings which would bring a man for miles
10 to see a coffin at which on his arrival he did not cast one passing glance. We came to the conclusion that the cause must be sought in this fact: that the Briton does not enjoy doing a thing so much as in the recollection of having done it; and perhaps some secrets of our great deeds as a nation be traced [*sic*] to this general attitude of the
15 British mind.

Others walked by with little children who were lifted up to gaze on the funeral pile. Some grandchildren of these little mites may be living in the year 2018 . . . .

18–20 June 1898

20 One night when our party had gone to bed I found myself alone with Mr. Chamberlain in the billiard room, and we fell to talking

about the monument to be erected in honour of Mr. Gladstone. From that we proceeded to talk of Mr. Gladstone and his work. Suddenly without warning, and certainly without provocation on
25 my part, Chamberlain poured forth invective with amazing freedom and warmth: I cannot remember all he said but he began by asking what policy Mr. Gladstone had initiated. His finance was Peel's; Bright was the real father of Reform. The Test Acts did not originate with him, nor did Home Rule. Then Mr. Gladstone
30 supported measures of which it is notorious that he disapproved – local veto, and the attack upon the church in Wales . . . .

'He never made a phrase that will live; he never wrote a book that has not been laughed out of print: and as for his foreign policy – well it was not mine.'

35 While admitting the personal charm of Mr. Gladstone, Chamberlain has (doubtless) good cause for reminding me that on certain occasions, especially when the Irish questions were being discussed, the aspect of the fiend took possession of Mr. Gladstone's face: and of course it was Chamberlain who most frequently courted
40 these angry flashes of gleaming wrath. 'It is his great age, and that alone which has called forth this man of sentimentalism . . . .'

Then followed a curious appreciation of Lord Beaconsfield 'whom I was brought up to hate, and whom I hated'. Chamberlain said frankly enough that his admiration of him would never be
45 great, but that his respect for him was always increasing. He was the founder of Tory democracy; he could convey his meaning in a direct phrase, and he had a foreign policy . . . . It was an interesting half hour and to some extent has changed my opinion about Joe.

The Crawford Papers, ed. John Vincent, 1984, pp 48–50 (David Lindsay, 27th Earl of Crawford, was later Unionist Chief Whip).

Questions

a What are the values and limitations of journal entries such as this for reconstructing opinions?

b Would you agree with Crawford that it was Gladstone's great age which had evoked sentimentalism at his death?

c Do we learn most from this extract about Gladstone, Disraeli, Chamberlain or the author?

